Biblical
Archaeology

Zondervan Quick-Reference Library

ZONDERVAN
QUICK
REFERENCE
LIBRARY

Biblical Archaeology

John H. Sailhamer

ZONDERVAN®

ZONDERVAN.com/
AUTHORTRACKER
follow your favorite authors

Biblical Archaeology
Copyright © 1998 by John H. Sailhamer

Requests for information should be addressed to:

Zondervan, *Grand Rapids, Michigan 49530*

Library of Congress Cataloging-in-Publication Data

Sailhamer, John
    Biblical archaeology / John H. Sailhamer.
        p.   cm. — (Zondervan quick reference library)
    ISBN: 0-310-20393-7 (softcover)
    ISBN: 978-0-310-20393-7 (softcover)
    1. Bible—Antiquities. 2. Bible—Evidences, authority, etc. 3. Bible O.T.—History of Biblical
events. I. Title. II. Series.
BS621.S25   1988
220.9′3—dc21   97-45993
                                                                                  CIP

Interior design by Sue Vandenberg Koppenol

Printed in the United States of America

98 99 00 01 02 03 04 • 10 9 8 7 6 5 4 3 2 1

Contents

Abbreviations

Books of the Bible

Genesis	Gen.	Mark	Mark
Exodus	Ex.	Luke	Luke
Leviticus	Lev.	John	John
Numbers	Num.	Acts	Acts
Deuteronomy	Deut.	Romans	Rom.
Joshua	Josh.	1 Corinthians	1 Cor.
Judges	Judg.	2 Corinthians	2 Cor.
Ruth	Ruth	Galatians	Gal.
1 Samuel	1 Sam.	Ephesians	Eph.
2 Samuel	2 Sam.	Philippians	Phil.
1 Kings	1 Kings	Colossians	Col.
2 Kings	2 Kings	1 Thessalonians	1 Thess.
1 Chronicles	1 Chron.	2 Thessalonians	2 Thess.
2 Chronicles	2 Chron.	1 Timothy	1 Tim.
Ezra	Ezra	2 Timothy	2 Tim.
Nehemiah	Neh.	Titus	Titus
Esther	Est.	Philemon	Philem.
Job	Job	Hebrews	Heb.
Psalms	Ps(s).	James	James
Proverbs	Prov.	1 Peter	1 Peter
Ecclesiastes	Eccl.	2 Peter	2 Peter
Song of Songs	Song	1 John	1 John
Isaiah	Isa.	2 John	2 John
Jeremiah	Jer.	3 John	3 John
Lamentations	Lam.	Jude	Jude
Ezekiel	Ezek.	Revelation	Rev.
Daniel	Dan.		
Hosea	Hos.		
Joel	Joel		
Amos	Amos		
Obadiah	Obad.		
Jonah	Jonah		
Micah	Mic.		
Nahum	Nah.		
Habakkuk	Hab.		
Zephaniah	Zeph.		
Haggai	Hag.		
Zechariah	Zech.		
Malachi	Mal.		
Matthew	Matt.		

Other Abbreviations

ANET — *Ancient Near Eastern Texts Relating to the Old Testament,* ed. James B. Pritchard

ANEP — *The Ancient Near East in Pictures Relating to the Old Testament,* ed. James B. Pritchard

TANE — *The Ancient Near East: An Anthology of Texts and Pictures,* ed. James B. Pritchard

Introduction

What Is This Book?

The *Zondervan Quick-Reference Library: Biblical Archaeology* is a new and unique reference tool. Simply put, it is a complete and succinct commentary on the prophetic element of the Bible; each unit of this discussion you can read approximately in one minute. You do not need to wade through a lot of information, for this book goes right to the point—the exposition of the major issues of biblical archaeology itself. It not only takes into account the latest in biblical scholarship, it also shows the relevance of biblical archaeology to the Bible.

Because we get so much of our information in daily life quickly and efficiently, we are becoming increasingly accustomed to having information or knowledge about the Bible given to us in the same way. Though the need for fast delivery systems often undercuts the role of thoughtful reflection in our society, our habits have changed. We have adjusted to the routines of everyday life around us. There is therefore a legitimate need for a more efficient way to build our knowledge of the Bible and its content—if only as a starting point for more in-depth and reflective understanding. It is a truism in learning that once we get a sense of what a particular Bible theme is about, the details of that theme make more sense.

A regular use of the *Zondervan Quick-Reference Library: Biblical Archaeology* should lead to a more knowledgeable study of God's Word. It can, of course, be used along with traditional Bible study tools, and this book is not intended to replace them. Rather, our aim is to supply the legitimate need (or appetite) for efficiency in obtaining Bible knowledge. It is a convenient starting point.

The *Zondervan Quick-Reference Library: Biblical Archaeology* has two distinct features: (1) a series of introductory pages, intended to bring the reader up to speed on the study of biblical archaeology; (2) a series of brief comments on all the major archaeological finds relevant to the Bible. Each page, which covers a single topic, is intended to be read on its own. The book as a whole may also be read consecutively to obtain a complete picture of how archaeology relates to the Bible.

What Is Biblical Archaeology?

Biblical archaeology is a branch of the science of archaeology. As a science, archaeology studies human remains. Its task includes procedures both of uncovering those remains and of interpreting their meaning. The various kinds of human remains can be classified under two basic categories:

- Artifacts, which are the nonliterary objects that are the product of human activity. These include isolated objects such as bones, weapons, pottery, and jewelry, as well as larger projects such as houses, streets, and city walls.
- Literary sources, which are written documents, usually uncovered along with, or associated with, artifactual remains. Written documents can survive in the form of monuments, ostraca (small pieces of broken pottery, often used as a writing surface), and papyri (an ancient form of paper).

Artifacts are usually more difficult to interpret than literary documents. If they are complete enough, the latter in large measure provide much of their own interpretation. Ancient writers, like modern ones, wrote to be understood. That does not mean, however, that we can always clearly understand the ancient languages of the biblical periods. We know a great deal about them, but more texts are being uncovered each year and much more must still be learned about those already discovered. The study of ancient languages and texts is called *philology*.

When it comes to the interpretation of artifactual evidence, the archaeologist has to rely on procedures and techniques of study that have evolved over the years. It is often difficult to interpret the raw data uncovered by the shovel. By itself a broken piece of pottery tells us little about the historical events of the day in which it was made. But this does not mean that such an artifact is useless for historical purposes. Archaeologists use various pottery styles to help in dating and identifying artifacts. We can know ancient cultures and people from the distinctive style of pottery they manufactured and used.

Moreover, since ancient cities were often destroyed in times of war and invasion, the various destruction levels uncovered at the site of an ancient city have also become a standard means for dating and identifying artifacts. Major historical events, such as the invasion of a land by a hostile power, often leave clear traces of destruction that can be further linked to other artifacts at the site of an ancient city. When both pottery styles and destruction levels at a specific site are linked to other cultural and literary remains, we can learn a significant amount about the lives of the ancient Near Eastern peoples who inhabited the lands of the Bible.

What Is the Contribution of Biblical Archaeology?

The science of archaeology has contributed to the study of the Bible in two important ways.

(1) Archaeology has produced a wealth of information relating to the world of the Bible. We probably know more about the ancient world than most of those who lived at that time. Such information has enabled students of the Bible to understand more fully the events about which the biblical writers wrote. We are still, of course, dependent on them for their interpretation of the events. They were inspired. But by means of the additional information about those events and places available through archaeology, we can view the Bible within a wide, and more ancient, perspective.

The patriarch Abraham, for example, looms large in the narratives of the Bible. The Bible recounts only those aspects of Abraham's life that relate to the specific message the author wanted to get across to his readers—Abraham's simple faith and trust in God. Many details of his life and culture are thus left out. Though not essential for understanding the biblical author's intent, archaeology can help fill in many of the details that lie behind the texts of Scripture.

Are such details important for better understanding the Bible? Some biblical scholars believe they are. We believe, however, that the biblical texts are sufficiently clear to the alert reader of the Bible. The authors give us enough information to interpret the texts. When, for example, God promised Abraham that he would one day become a great nation, Abraham asked for a sign (Gen. 15:8). God gave him a sign in the form of a rather strange ceremony, in which animals were cut in two and laid along a pathway. God then sent a burning light to pass between the animals' parts (15:9–17). Biblical scholars have often sought to explain this ceremony by referring to similar ceremonies in the ancient world. Though such a procedure may help explain what the custom meant to Abraham within the context of his world, we should be careful not to let such general information influence the meaning that the biblical author intended. The author in this case has fortunately given us his own inspired interpretation of the strange custom. In the very next verse he informs us that in sending a burning light through the pieces of the slain animals, "the LORD made a covenant with Abram" (15:18). If we had not been told that this was a covenant ceremony, it is doubtful we would know it from archaeology.

(2) The science of archaeology has helped to demonstrate the historical reliability and trustworthiness of the Bible. Before the rise of the study of biblical archaeology, we really had little means for testing the accuracy of the Bible. The Bible was assumed to be true merely because it was accepted as God's Word. Archaeology has provided a much-needed tool for testing the Bible's own trustworthiness in recounting events from the ancient past.

Is the Bible Historically Reliable?

Beginning some two centuries ago, the Bible has been submitted to an increasingly closer critical attack on its historical reliability, particularly in recounting past events. The biblical authors, some scholars began to argue, were products of an ancient world vastly different from our own, in which little attention was given to the careful use of historical sources. In the absence of actual records from the past, these scholars assumed that ancient men such as Moses or Joshua could not have known how to write or would not have had access to ancient documents. They would not even have had an alphabet, it was argued. Such scholars also held that most of the narratives in the early parts of the Bible were simply later stories that had been told and retold and often embellished. Because they had never heard of such ancient people as the "Hittites" and the "Horites" from other sources, they assumed that the biblical authors merely made them up.

Many examples of alleged historical inaccuracies in the Bible have been overturned by the discoveries of biblical archaeology. For example, texts written in ancient Canaanite, the language of the Old Testament books, are now widely attested from the very century in which Moses lived and even much earlier. Such texts, written in an alphabetic script, prove beyond doubt that language flourished in Canaan long before Moses and Israel entered the land and long before the Bible began to be written. Excavations near the modern Turkish village of Bogaskoy have uncovered thousands of ancient documents from the ancient capital of a major kingdom of the Hittite people, who once controlled an empire that extended into the land of Palestine.

In one celebrated case of skepticism of the historical accuracy of the Bible, historians frequently referred to the Babylonian king Belshazzar, mentioned in Daniel 5. The Bible, they asserted, was wrong in identifying him as the last king of Babylon. Not only was he not the last king, but because there was no other mention of this king in ancient documents, they argued that he was only a figment of the biblical writer's imagination. But ancient texts uncovered in this century from the last days of the Babylonian empire do mention Belshazzar by name. True, those texts identify Belshazzar's father, Nabonidus, as the last king of Babylon. Is the Bible therefore still in error about the details of history? Once again, new discoveries have proved otherwise. We now know from ancient Babylonian records that Nabonidus fled Babylon in the last years of his reign and left his son Belshazzar to rule the city. In major and minor historical details, the science of archaeology has shown the Bible to be historically accurate.

What Is the Relationship
Between the Bible and Archaeology?

Both archaeology and the Bible give us a view of the past, and as noted, the former has often come to the defense of the latter. But what happens when the biblical account and the results of archaeology seem to conflict? We should keep in mind several considerations.

First, much of the biblical material is not likely to be attested in direct artifactual or inscriptional evidence. We should not expect to find, for example, an actual artifact from the household of a biblical character such as Abraham. Articles such as clothing and footwear are, for the most part, perishable. Ancient people often wrote on wax tablets and papyrus paper, and there is little hope that many of such texts have survived the elements.

Moreover, most of the biblical stories are about the lives of ordinary individuals who have likely left little trace of their lives. At the most, archaeology can tell us about the times in which such individuals lived. Most findings relate to kings and other rulers.

True, certain people, such as King Solomon, were prominent. In such cases, we might expect to find ample traces, both artifactual and inscriptional, of their lives. But in attempting to correlate the biblical material with the results of archaeology, only a small fraction of the ancient sites have actually been identified and excavated. Even when a site has been identified, it is never entirely dug up. The vast majority of most ancient biblical sites are deliberately left untouched for a future generation of archaeologists, in the hope that better methods and tools will be developed. The history of the science of archaeology is rife with examples of precious artifactual remains being pillaged, not only by grave robbers and fortune hunters, but also by well-meaning archaeologists using primitive methods.

Finally, surprisingly little of the material that is excavated ever gets catalogued and published and thus becomes available for analysis. The basements of most major museums around the world are filled with crates of artifactual remains unearthed decades ago. Such materials must be closely examined, catalogued, and studied in context with the total picture that slowly emerges from the analysis of an archaeological excavation. And many archaeologists are rightly hesitant to release the results of their excavations before all the data has been carefully sifted. The danger of a hasty misinterpretation is too great. The above factors serve to caution against drawing final conclusions about the Bible and archaeology before all the facts are in.

Biblical Archaeology and Interpretation

Both the Bible and the results of archaeological excavations are in need of a formidable amount of interpretation. There are few brute facts awaiting to be discovered, either in the pages of Scripture or in the ruins of an ancient city. For the most part, what is written in the Bible, though clear enough to the average reader, must undergo a fair amount of interpretation before one can say with certainty that one understands what it means.

We must keep in mind too that the biblical historical narratives are selective in their account of past events. The book of Judges, for example, covers over three hundred years, yet it recounts the lives of only twelve individuals. The book of Exodus skips over most of the events in the life of Israel for over four hundred years. According to archaeological inscriptions, the Israelite king Omri was one of the most powerful and influential kings of the northern kingdom, yet the biblical writer devotes no more than six verses to his reign. He was not interested in the social and political aspects of Omri's reign—only the spiritual dimensions.

Moreover, we must ask whether the dates and numbers in the Bible are to be taken literally, so that they can be used to establish a chronology for relating biblical events to ancient history. If, for example, we understand the chronological note in 1 Kings 6:1 as a valid reference point for dating the time of Israel's exodus from Egypt, then this event must lie within the fifteenth century B.C., and not the thirteenth century, as most archaeologists put it.

Archaeological material must also be sifted, weighed, and analyzed. Ultimately it must be placed within the larger historical and social context within which it is found. Yet artifacts are notoriously opaque and ambiguous. A simple piece of jewelry or pottery may serve to date an archaeological site and tell us something of its culture, but how do we know whether that artifact may have been an ancient heirloom, thus telling us little about the site where it was discovered.

Inscriptions too require interpretation. Their language and style must be studied and assessed according to their particular literary type or genre. The famous "law code" of the Babylonian king Hammurapi, for example, is today no longer consider a "code" of laws, but a "set" of examples of the wise decisions made by this king. If such is the case, then its value for biblical studies lies not in what it tells us about biblical laws, but about the biblical wisdom books such as Proverbs.

In the last analysis, both the Bible and archaeology focus on the work of human beings. Thus, we must always interpret them and explain what they mean. Moreover, though at any one time we may confidently say we understand them, our interpretation can never be final. It must always remain open to new discoveries.

Ancient Near Eastern Geography

The world of the ancient Near East is composed of two great river basins (the Nile and the Tigris–Euphrates), a coastline, a range of mountains, and a large desert. The Nile River originates in East Africa and Ethiopia and drains into the southern Mediterranean Sea. Its waters annually bring rich soil deposits from the rain forests and melting snows of Africa. As the river overflows its banks, the waters of the Nile spread a layer of fertile soil over the Nile valley. On both sides of the Nile, high desert plateaus stretch—into Arabia on the east and Libya on the west. The narrow strip of fertile farmland became the home of a powerful world empire—Egypt.

The Mesopotamian valley was home to a series of powerful ancient empires. The Tigris and Euphrates Rivers both originate in the mountains of Armenia and empty into the Persian Gulf. Like the Nile, they flow through an arid, rainless plain and are bordered on the west by the Arabian Desert and on the east by the high mountain ranges of Iran. Each year, these two mighty rivers also overflow their banks and inundate their valleys with rich fertile soil. Thus along these two rivers human societies developed that were able to take advantage of the abundant farmlands and ultimately to control the seasonal floods with man-made irrigation systems.

The coastline of the ancient Near East was the narrow strip of land along the eastern Mediterranean Sea—a region known as Syria and Palestine (its ancient name was Canaan). This region consists of a series of low mountain ranges divided from north to south by a massive geological rift. To the far north, the Orontes River flows through this rift. Further south, the Jordan River flows through the same rift and empties into the Dead Sea. In the far south, the rift opens up into the Red Sea and resurfaces again along the eastern coastline of Africa. Unlike the arid river basins of Egypt and Mesopotamia, Syria-Palestine receives an ample yearly rainfall.

To the far east of that region, however, the air becomes arid again and the rains cease, leaving the massive Arabian Desert on its eastern border. That region is humanly uninhabitable. Stretching across the north and east of Syria and Mesopotamia are a series of high mountain ranges, known in the ancient world as the Zagros Mountains. The western edge opened into Asia Minor; in the north lay Armenia, and in the southeast the mountains of Iran.

Because the inhabitable lands fell along the two river basins to the west and east and the Mediterranean coastline in the center, the entire area is known as the Fertile Crescent. Here human beings could plant crops, enjoy ample water supplies, and establish sizable enough cities to house the necessary workers and administrators to maintain their irrigation projects. In this Fertile Crescent the major events of world history and biblical history transpired.

Ancient Near Eastern Chronology (Egypt)

Biblical archaeology is a branch of the broader study of ancient Near Eastern history and archaeology. It is thus helpful to review its historical and archaeological periods.

We begin with a survey of the kingdoms and dynasties of Egypt. The first great period of Egyptian history was one of a highly centralized and ordered government. This was the period of the Old Kingdom (29th–23d centuries B.C.). The high point of this period in Egyptian history centered around the third and the fourth dynasties, during which time the great pyramids of Egypt were built. The famous "Step-Pyramid" of King Djoser, the Sphinx, and the pyramids of Giza were all built about 2700 B.C. The largest of the pyramids, that of King Cheops, is some 485 feet high. The pyramids are a testimony to large and prosperous kingdoms that ruled in Egypt.

The Old Kingdom was followed by a time of general decline in prosperity and order—a period known as the First Intermediate Period. It represented the seventh to the eleventh dynasties (22d–20th centuries B.C.).

The second great period of Egyptian history, the Middle Kingdom, consisted primarily of the twelfth dynasty (late 20th–18th century B.C.). This was the classical period of Egyptian culture, art, and literature. During this period Joseph and his brothers entered Egypt. Following the Middle Kingdom, Egypt was invaded by a foreign people known as the Hyksos—a time known as the Second Intermediate Period (18th–16th centuries B.C.). That period was followed by the New Kingdom—a time of imperialistic expansion across the borders of its southern and northern neighbors, which began about 1550 B.C., when the Egyptians overthrew the Hyksos and drove them out of their land. At about the same time, the Egyptians, under the control of the great kings of the eighteenth dynasty, gained control of a large part of Palestine and Syria. After the infamous rule of Rameses II of the nineteenth dynasty, the glory of the Egyption empire began to fade. For most of its later history, Egypt played a minor role in international world affairs.

Ancient Near Eastern Chronology (Mesopotamia)

In the earliest stages of civilization in Mesopotamia (4th–3d millennia B.C.), a group of people known as the Sumerians lived in small city-states around the city of Nippur in southern Mesopotamia. During the middle of the third millennium, a group of Semitic people living among the Sumerians rose to power and founded their own empire in northern Mesopotamia. This was the Akkad Empire, ruled by King Sargon. Sargon's empire lasted only a century and a half. It fell to a newly established Sumerian dynasty in the southern Mesopotamian city of Ur. That Sumerian dynasty, known as Ur III, lasted from 2060 to 1950 B.C.

This dynasty apparently collapsed in the face of a huge influx of West Semitic immigrants from the fringes of the Arabian Desert, who gained control of much of southern Mesopotamia and established a series of small kingdoms. One of those kingdoms, centered in the city of Babylon and led by the powerful King Hammurapi (1728–1686 B.C.), united the other kingdoms of southern Mesopotamia and extended its rule to the north. Babylon was a major political force in Mesopotamia until the rise of the Assyrian empire in the north. This happened primarily during the Middle Assyrian period (14th–13th century B.C.). The high point of Assyrian influence came during the New Assyrian Kingdom (935–612 B.C.), during which time the Assyrians ruled nearly all of Mesopotamia, parts of Asia Minor, and all of Syria and Palestine. Their rule even extended into Egypt.

In 612 B.C., the Assyrian capital city of Nineveh was defeated by the armies of the Medes and the Neo-Babylonians. During the time of the decline of Assyria, the Neo-Babylonian (that is, Chaldean) Kingdom was founded in southern Mesopotamia (625–539 B.C.). The most notorious king of that kingdom was Nebuchadnezzar. In 539 B.C., Babylon was conquered by the Persian King Cyrus. Persian rule continued through the Near East until 331 B.C., when it was replaced by the Greek empire of Alexander the Great.

The History of Syria-Palestine (Land of the Bible)

The earliest period in which we are interested in Syria-Palestine is called the Early Bronze Age (3300–2300 B.C.)—a time when tools and weapons were made from bronze. Archaeologists mark cultural periods by the materials used in making tools and weapons. This period is marked by a series of invasions by a diverse group of peoples. These new populations were the ancestors of the Canaanites, who lived in Palestine during the biblical period. They built great cities throughout the land. Characteristic of these cities were the massive walls surrounding them—some as thick as thirty feet wide.

Some time after 2300 B.C., Palestine experienced a catastrophic invasion or uprising in which all the cities built during the Early Bronze Age were destroyed. For a period of time, the cities in Palestine continued to lay in ruins; few archaeological remains have been found of this period. What is known about it comes primarily from gravesites. The fact that graves exhibit totally new burial practices has led to the conclusion that a new group of people entered Palestine—first as invaders and then as migrating families. From all appearances, they were a pastoral people, who lived in broadly defined tribal groups. The time they lived in Palestine is known as the Early Bronze–Middle Bronze Transition Period (2300–1900 B.C.).

At the end of this transitional stage, these immigrants began to build permanent settlements in Palestine. During the next several centuries (Middle Bronze Age, 1900–1550 B.C.), new waves of Indo-Aryan, non-Semitic peoples, the "Horites" of the biblical narratives, migrated into Palestine, bringing with them a powerful new weapon, the horse-drawn chariot. In the seventeenth century B.C., Palestine was the center of a Semitic empire controlled by the Hyksos in Egypt. This empire was ruled by numerous local chieftains, who were constantly at war with each other. At the end of the Hyksos rule in Egypt (1550 B.C.), Palestine was conquered and controlled by the Egyptian kings of the eighteenth and nineteenth dynasties.

During the Late Bronze Age (1500–1200 B.C.), biblical Israel comes into the picture. After leaving Egypt in 1400 B.C. and wandering for forty years in the desert, the Israelites entered Palestine. A short time of warfare followed their entry into the land. This was the time of the Conquest, under the leadership of Joshua (ca. 1400 B.C.). The Bible is not clear on the length of the Conquest, but most agree it could not have been longer than ten or fifteen years. During the next three hundred years, however (the time covered by the book of Judges), control of Palestine exchanged hands many times. In the latter years of that period and during the days of the United Monarchy, the Iron Age was ushered into Palestine (ca. 1200 B.C.). Iron became the characteristic material from which tools and weapons were made. The Iron Age lasted in Palestine throughout the remainder of the biblical period.

Archaeology and Genesis 1–11

Introduction

Archaeologically speaking, the first eleven chapters of Genesis form a period distinct from the rest of the biblical narratives. The subject matter of these chapters is not limited to Israel and the land of Palestine, but is concerned with events of a global scale—Creation, the Flood, and the rise and fall of civilizations. Because of the vast scope of these chapters, archaeology in itself will probably never directly shed much light on those events. Questions about Creation and the Flood, in fact, belong to the science of astronomy and geology.

It is possible, however, to reconstruct a general picture of the early stages of human civilization and the world and to view these chapters from within that perspective. There is no complete agreement among evangelical Christians on this issue apart from the biblical account. They divide into two distinct approaches. Those who basically accept the views of modern archaeologists and anthropologists attempt to correlate the biblical narratives with that view. Others, however, hold that the modern scientific view of early human society is fundamentally flawed. They argue that we must take into account the biblical view if we are to understand the origin of our world and human societies. The biblical account of the Flood, they argue, would have radically affected human life and geological conditions on earth.

We believe neither of the two views gives an adequate picture of the real world. While the modern scientific picture of early human beings is quite different than what we find in the Bible, it is also true that much of what the modern archaeologist says about early human beings is derived not from the evidence itself but from an essentially unbiblical set of assumptions—for example, that "early humans" evolved from primitive, "prehuman" lower forms of animal life.

But the Bible knows of no such state of affairs. It pictures the first man and woman as fully human, capable of complex cultural skills such as language, farming, and raising livestock. There was nothing "primitive" about Adam and Eve as far as their culture is concerned. They lived much the same as many societies today. They were not, of course, technologically advanced, but neither were they "primitive." When we hear archaeologists speaking of genuinely human remains, we should think of them as descendants of Adam and Eve. It is only by assuming a need for early "primitive" humans to develop into the more advanced stages that archaeologists are forced to assume lengthy time periods (above 50,000 years ago) for early humans. Care must also be taken not to confuse the scientific evidence for "early humans," descendants of Adam, with the remains of earlier forms of animal life, such as chimpanzees and apes.

A General Picture of Early Human Society

Archaeologists classify early human cultures by the materials they used for making tools and weapons. The earliest human societies used stone implements—hence the Stone Age. The Old Stone Age, or Paleolithic, culture lasted from about 50,000 to 10,000 B.C. During that period, food was gathered from wild plants and hunting. At around 9,000 B.C. human culture entered a rather sudden transitional phase, the Mesolithic, or Middle Stone Age, when many human cultures ceased depending on hunting and gathering food and began the process of domesticating plants and animals.

The chief cause of this transition in basic economies was a dramatic change in global climatic conditions. As temperatures began to rise at the close of the last Ice Age, large areas of land were left exposed to the warm climate. Vast forests rapidly covered the landscape. Paleolithic societies, which had once thrived on hunting large herds of reindeer, now found themselves having to stalk deer in densely forested terrain. Only by refining their tools and hunting implements (such as the bow and arrow, with finely tooled stone arrow tips) were people able to survive. The domestication of the dog also added to their hunting capacities.

The biblical city of Jericho provides a textbook picture of the progress of human culture throughout the early stages of prehistory. From the time of its early Mesolithic inhabitants, it was almost constantly occupied until the Israelites destroyed it in their conquest of Canaan. A Mesolithic culture flourished until its destruction in 7800 B.C. Its early inhabitants lived in modest mud huts at the top of an ancient hill at the center of the city. The technological revolution of domesticated plants and animals led directly to the Neolithic, or New Stone Age culture. This period began with the destruction of the huts of the earlier Mesolithic culture. An estimated two thousand inhabitants now lived in mud huts surrounded by a formidable city wall. At the corner of the west end of the city wall they constructed a large tower to help them defend the city. The only identifiable domesticated animal at that time was the goat.

The early Neolithic people of Jericho occupied the city for nearly a thousand years. After a short period when the city was deserted, a new population moved onto the hill. These new inhabitants still hunted wild animals for food, but they had also domesticated several kinds of animals and raised their own crops. They were part of a larger group of people living in settlements throughout ancient Palestine.

After another brief period of abandonment, a new population moved into Palestine around 6,000 B.C. and took up residence in Jericho. These people brought with them a highly developed use of pottery, domesticated livestock, and agricultural skills. In 4500 B.C. the first traces of metal tools were deposited in gravesites near Jericho. The city, however, remained unoccupied until another new population entered Palestine in 3100 B.C. and initiated an urbanized Early Bronze Age culture in Palestine.

Ancient Near Eastern Creation Accounts

Strictly speaking, there are no known creation accounts from the ancient Near East. There are, to be sure, several ancient myths from both Egypt and Mesopotamia that give accounts of creation in varying degrees and for different purposes. But there is no actual narrative account of creation, such as the one we find at the beginning of the Bible. Outside that biblical account, creation was not so much a fact from the past as it was an idea about the present. Ancient creation myths were designed to explain why things happen in the world today as they do.

The most notable ancient creation myth is the epic poem known to the Babylonians and Assyrians as *Enuma Elish*. Its title is taken from the first words of the epic, which begins, "When on high (*enuma elish*) the heaven had not been named, firm ground below had not been called by name. . . ." Since the first discovery of ancient fragments of clay tablets recounting the epic (1848–1876), *Enuma Elish* has been studied as an ancient account of creation that bears surprising similarity to the Genesis account. In actual fact, creation plays a relatively minor role in the epic. Central to the epic is the attempt to explain why the Babylonian god Marduk is to be revered as the chief among the gods. The epic probably dates only from the time of the earliest copies of the epic (ca. 1,000 B.C.), though it may be older than that.

Enuma Elish begins by describing a primordial time when nothing yet existed except the three gods: Apsu (the primeval fresh water ocean), Tiamat (the salt water ocean), and their son, Mummu (the mist). In these three gods were represented all the elements of which the universe was thought to consist. As the epic story progresses, Apsu and Tiamat give birth to a multitude of gods. But a problem develops. The noise created by these younger gods begin to get on the nerves of the original pair. Apsu, taking matters into his own hands, decides to destroy the other gods and thus rest in silence. But his plan is thwarted by the god Ea, who casts a spell on Apsu, puts him into a deep sleep, and slays him in his sleep. Tiamat, understandably, is greatly disturbed by the death of her husband and sets out on a plan to avenge his death.

No one can contain Tiamat's rage against the other gods until the Babylonian chief deity, Marduk, is summoned to the fight. But he cleverly refuses to fight Tiamat until all the gods have pledged to make him the supreme god. When the gods agree to this, Marduk wages war with Tiamat. In the account of his slaying of Tiamat the story of creation is told. Standing over the slain Tiamat, Marduk "split her like a shellfish into two parts: Half of her he set up and ceiled it as sky"; with the other half he constructs an abode for the surviving gods. When the lesser gods complain of the work they are assigned, Marduk creates human beings to serve them.

At the conclusion of the epic, Marduk is awarded a city and a temple, built for him by the council of gods. That city is Babylon, with its great temple. Isn't it interesting that the biblical account of Creation also concludes in Genesis 11:1–9 with an account of the building of the city of Babylon? The Bible, however, as might be expected, has a quite different assessment of that city. Babylon is not the "gateway to heaven," as ancient mythology supposed. Rather, it is the origin of all human futility and rebellion against God. In the biblical story, the name Babylon is identified with the "confusion" of languages that lies at the heart of all human misunderstanding.

Ancient Near Eastern Myth of the Garden of Eden

Apparently people in the ancient Near East believed in an early, earthly paradise, a place where all the woes and ills of this present life had not yet obtained. Such views are, in a few details, remarkably similar to the biblical account of the Garden of Eden. In an early Sumerian myth, *Enki and Ninhursag* (*ANET*, pp. 37–41), for example, a "land" called Dilmun is described as "clean and bright [where] . . . the lion kills not, the wolf snatches not the lamb, unknown is the kid-devouring wild dog." It is a place where "the old man (says) not, 'I am an old man,'" and where a constantly flowing river brings great abundance to the city that lies in its midst.

There are clear similarities here with the biblical account of Eden. But it should be noted that the Genesis account of the Garden of Eden does not suggests that lions did not kill or wolves did not snatch helpless lambs. That, of course, is true of other biblical pictures of paradise (such as Isa. 65:25), but it is not found in Genesis 2.

Ancient Near Eastern Myths
of the Creation of Human Beings

Curiously, in *Enki and Ninhursag,* a Sumerion myth discussed in the previous pages, a goddess named Ninhursag creates the goddess of life, Ninti, to soothe the hurting "rib" of her brother, Enki. The mention of a "rib" in conjunction with the creation of a female goddess has led some to compare this story with the biblical account of the creation of Eve from Adam's "rib." In the Sumerian myth, however, the mention of Enki's "rib" occurs in a long lists of other body parts that "hurt" Enki and for which Ninhursag creates numerous gods to heal him. The mention of the "rib" is thus not as striking as might first appear.

As in the Bible, in some Babylonian and Sumerian myths human beings are created from the ground. Sometimes their creation is pictured as a plant growing out of the ground, and other times as a clay figurine molded by a potter. In the Babylonian account *Atrahasis*, for example, humankind is created from the blood of a slain god mixed with clay. Human beings are thus depicted as clay figurines filled with divine blood. It is often argued that this view of the creation of human beings bears remarkable similarity to the biblical account of God's "fashioning" man from the dust of the ground (Gen. 2:7).

But one must recognize a fundamental difference in literary type between the ancient Babylonian account and the Bible. *Atrahasis* is an epic poem; the Bible is written as historical narrative. The depiction of human beings as clay figurines is a poetic image. The Bible, on the other hand, gives a straightforward account of the man Adam's creation from the ground. In the Bible, the Hebrew word used to recount God's "fashioning" a man (Gen. 2:7) is related to the word for "potter." That has seemed to many to make its relationship to *Atrahasis* virtually certain. More recently, however, two important factors have suggested that the biblical account is quite different than the Babylonian one. (1) We now know that the Hebrew word often translated "to fashion" in Genesis 2:7 means simply "to create." There is thus nothing in that Hebrew word to suggest the image of a potter. (2) The text of 2:7 does not use the word for "clay," as one would expect if the sense were of a potter making a figurine. The word used is simply "dirt" or "soil." The biblical account is interested in where the man came from, not what he is made of.

To be sure, biblical poetry frequently envisions human beings as "houses of clay" (Job 4:19) and God as our "potter" (Isa. 29:16), but there is a vast difference between a poetic image and an historical narrative account. The similarities between the biblical view of humanity and that of the ancient Near East lies in their use of common poetic images—not in their understanding of humankind's origins.

Ancient Near Eastern Flood Accounts

No other biblical passage has so many extrabiblical parallels as does the Genesis account of the Flood. More than three hundred "flood texts" from around the world have been collected and published. Those texts record ancient and primitive accounts of a worldwide flood and the survival of a single man and his family. There are many other similarities, both among these documents and with the biblical story of the Flood.

The single most important Flood story from the ancient world is found in the *Epic of Gilgamesh*. This epic is about a man's quest for eternal life, and the story of the Flood is one of its chapters. Gilgamesh, the hero of the epic and a kind of ancient Marco Polo, sets out on a long search to meet the famous survivor of the Flood, Utnapishtum. He of all persons, Gilgamesh believes, will know the secret of immortality—Utnapishtum was granted immortality by surviving the Flood. When Gilgamesh finally meets him, he hears the harrowing account of the Flood and of Utnapishtum's survival.

One day, while living peacefully in a city on the banks of the Euphrates River, Utnapishtum was warned by the god Ninigiku-Ea of a devastating flood that the other gods had decided to send against the city. Utnapishtum was warned to tear down his house and build a ship. The god gave him the dimensions of the ship he was to build and further instructed him to take aboard the ship "the seed of all living things." The ship itself was to be in the shape of a huge square box, sealed with asphalt and stocked with a great amount of food. After seven days, the ship was launched into the Euphrates River, and Utnapishtum brought abroad all his family and every craftsman of the city, along with "the beasts of the field [and] the wild creatures." When it began to rain, he boarded the ship and "battened up the entrance." Then followed a frightening storm and flood. Humankind was devastated, engulfed by the flood. Even "the gods were frightened by the deluge." They fled into heaven and "cowered like dogs, crouched against the outer wall." They lamented the destruction they had brought on the very people they had created. "The gods, all humbled, sit and weep."

The rains lasted seven days. When Utnapishtum looked out at the devastation, he saw that "all of mankind had returned to clay" and wept at the sight. In time, the ship rested on a high mountain, Mount Nisir. After seven days, Utnapishtum sent out a dove, but it returned, having found no resting place on dry land. He then sent out a swallow, and it too returned. He then sent a raven, and it did not return. At that, Utnapishtum and all those with him on the ship disembarked and immediately "offered a sacrifice." The gods were appeased, and a jewel necklace of lapis lazuli was given to the goddess Ishtar as a reminder "of these days, forgetting (them) never."

When the god Enlil, who had brought on this flood, found the ship and the survivors, he flew into a rage. "No man was to survive the destruction!"

he told the other gods. Enlil was then persuaded by the other gods that it was Utnapishtum's own wisdom that enabled him to anticipate and survive the deluge. At that, Enlil awarded Utnapishtum and his wife the immortality of the gods, and he was given a home "far away, at the mouth of the rivers."

The complete copies of this epic date from the seventh century B.C. Fragments of it date from the eighteenth century B.C. It is reasonable to suppose that the epic itself dates back to about 2,000 B.C. It is also fairly certain that the story of Utnapishtum and the Flood, which is only a part of the epic, is much older than the epic itself.

Another Babylonian version of the flood story is called the *Atrahasis Epic*. It also includes an account of the creation of humanity (see previous unit), dates from the early second millennium B.C., and probably served as the basis of the account in the *Gilgamesh Epic* (see page 31).

The Genealogy of Genesis 5

The genealogy of Genesis 5 contains a record of the families of ten great men who lived before the Flood. It begins with Adam and concludes with Noah, the survivor of the Flood. Each individual is credited with a large number of years, reaching ages of nearly 1,000 years. One individual, Enoch, is given special mention because God "took him away" (Gen. 5:24).

In an earlier age, this genealogy was understood to be not only a list of great men, but also a precise chronology of the early biblical period. On the basis of the ages of the ten men, scholars calculated that Adam was created only about 4000 years before the birth of Christ. Careful observation of other biblical genealogies have suggested, however, that they were not intended to provide chronologies. Such lists in the Bible often omit vast periods of time between important individuals. There is no certain way to obtain a figure for the total time between Adam and Noah. The individuals belong to the time period we must continue to call "prehistoric" (or "preflood").

The ancient Near East has several examples of such lists of ten (or less) great individuals. In his famous *History of Babylon*, the third-century B.C. Babylonian priest Berosus recorded a list of ten such men. Scholars have carefully studied this list, particularly its similarities to the Bible. The individuals in the list, for example, show large numbers of years for their ages. Attempts have been made to correlate the names in Berosus's list with those in Genesis 5. The name "Amelon" in Berosus's list, for example, has been related to the Babylonian term for "man" (*amelu*). That, in turn, has been identified with the Hebrew name Enosh, which means "man" in Hebrew. The name "Ammenon" has been identified with the Babylonian term *ummanu*, which means "builder," and has been linked to the biblical name "Kenan," which also means "builder."

Such similarities were based on the assumption that a Babylonian version lay behind Berosus's list. We now know, thanks to recent discoveries, that the original list was not written in ancient Babylonian, but in ancient Sumerian. When the names in this list are read as Sumerian words, the similarities with Genesis 5 largely disappear. What is significant, however, is the fact the Sumerian version of ten great names, which ultimately lay behind Berosus's list, once served as part of a larger Sumerian story of the Flood— just as in the Bible. In the Sumerian story, each individual lived a lengthy number of years. The first man in the list, for example, is said to have reigned 28,800 years as king of the Sumerian city of Eridu. Three of the kings listed reigned a total of 108,000 years. After the Flood, the reign of Sumerian kings takes on more biblical proportions, ranging from about 1,200 years down to a couple hundred years. At least in this general regard, the long lives of the Sumerian kings resembles the long lives of the ten men in the Bible from

Adam to Noah. The fact that the length of years drops dramatically after the Flood also parallels the biblical data.

Behind the long ages of the great men before the Flood, both in the Bible and at Sumer, there most likely lies a complex code or system in which numbers had a symbolic as well as real value. The large numbers in the Sumerian list are intended to show that the early kingship originated with men whose long lives marked them as favored by the gods. The large numbers in Genesis 5, on the other hand, are intended to show that human beings before the Flood were not gods, and though they lived many years, their lives always ended before they reached a thousand years. The point of Genesis 5 is not how long these men lived, but that they all, except Enoch, died as a result of Adam's fall.

Enoch was the seventh individual from Adam. He did not die, but was taken to be with God because "he walked with God." The seventh individual in the Babylonian tradition was also a privileged person. According to Babylonian mythology, Enmeduranki was made an associate of the gods, given a golden throne, and allowed to know the secrets of the gods.

The Bible and the ancient Near East thus appear to share a similar view of the time before the great Flood. As the biblical writer puts it, these were times when great men, "men of reknown" (Gen. 6:4), roamed the earth and made names for themselves. Whereas the ancient Near East versions of the stories of these men put them in a positive light, the Bible looks upon them with less favor. They, like all the other descendants of Adam, met their destiny in the consequences of the Fall. Only two, Enoch and Noah, who both walked with God, found grace in his sight. Such a perspective on the lives of early humankind is markedly different from that of the ancient Near East documents.

The Genesis Flood and the Babylonian Accounts

The marked similarities between the *Gilgamesh* and *Atrahasis Epics* demonstrate a general consensus in the ancient Near Eastern cultures concerning an ancient worldwide flood. This consensus consisted of several basic elements that were adapted and refashioned to fit each particular cultural and literary context. The biblical account seems also to be a part of this common tradition. The question is: How is the Genesis account related to the other accounts? Did the biblical authors borrow parts of ancient Flood stories? Did the ancient Babylonian poets draw from the basic story of the Bible? Did both the biblical authors and the Babylonian poets rely on earlier, more ancient versions of the story?

(1) All ancient accounts of the Flood differ greatly in their basic theological perspective. Not only does the marked theistic view of the biblical account differ fundamentally from the ancient Near Eastern accounts, but those accounts themselves differ greatly among themselves.

(2) Recent comparative studies of ancient accounts of the Flood suggest that an early Flood story once enjoyed worldwide circulation. A version of such an account has been identified in the Greek flood story of Apollodorus, in which the Greek god Zeus both sends the Flood to destroy humankind and rescues the sole survivor. That is a far cry from the Babylonian accounts, in which the Flood was determined by the decision of a council of gods, while humankind is rescued by another, more sympathetic god. Such comparisons suggest that the Genesis Flood story represents an original nonmythological version and that the Babylonian and Sumerian versions are later adaptations.

(3) Insofar as Flood stories (each following the same basic pattern) survive everywhere—as early as 1500 B.C. in India, for example—an original Flood account must have circulated. Though many versions have cultural and magical features, together they represent a form of the story that existed before the mythological accounts developed. In comparing all such stories, the biblical story of Noah clearly exhibits a premythological stage preceding the known ancient accounts. Moreover, it is also reasonable to conclude that the biblical account lies closest to that great catastrophe that rests at the base of the collective memory of humankind.

How does archaeology relate to the actual remains of the biblical flood? If one holds to a local flood, then archaeologists may one day uncover the remains of such a devastating deluge. The British archaeologist Sir Leonard Woolley, in fact, once believed he had uncovered the remains of the biblical flood in an eight-foot layer of clay covering the ancient Sumerian city of Ur. But there were several such layers at Ur, and thus none of them could lay claim to being *the* biblical flood. If one holds, however, to a universal flood, then it would not be likely that an archaeologist would find traces of such a large scale event. One would have to turn to the geologist for evidence.

The City (Tower) of Babylon (Babel)

Genesis 1–11 concludes with an account of the building of the city of Babylon and a tower. Unfortunately English translators have rendered the name of the city as "Babel"—a word that is, in fact, the Hebrew name for "Babylon." Thus they have veiled the central theme of the story, which is about the founding of Babylon. As the Genesis narrator sees it, this city is the first large-scale human effort to oppose God's plan of blessing for all humanity. It is, as it were, the "antichrist." What God intended to do in creation, humankind took upon themselves to do in the city of Babylon. The thread of biblical narrative runs from creation (Gen. 1) to the Fall (Gen. 3) and then to the building of the city of Babylon (Gen. 11). Babylon is a biblical image for all that is wrong with the human race.

Given the similarities between the biblical texts and ancient Near Eastern traditions, it seems hardly accidental that the Babylonian creation account, *Enuma Elish*, also concludes with an account of the founding of Babylon. In that case, however, Babylon is not the antichrist but the abode of the high God, Marduk. After seeing him create the world, the gods gathered around him and said, "Construct Babylon. . . . Let its brickwork be fashioned. You shall name it 'The Sanctuary.'" They "molded bricks" for the city, built a tower, and "set up in it an abode for Marduk." When it was completed, they proclaimed to Marduk, "This is Babylon, the place that is your home!" They then pronounced the fifty names of Marduk over the city and its temple tower.

The biblical narrator has, of course, a different view of the founding of Babylon. The "name" they call upon the city is not one that praises the god Marduk but is "City of Confusion." Here the biblical author makes a wordplay on the Babylonian name in Hebrew and comes up with the comical name "Babble." It is as if we would call it today, the "City of Babble-on."

Genesis 11 also contains a brief introductory description of an earlier time when "the whole land [or earth] spoke one language." The many human languages, the Bible implies, stem in large part from the confusion of tongues at Babylon. A remarkably parallel account exists in an early Sumerian epic entitled *Enmerkar and the Lord of Aratta*, in which the Sumerian god Enki "changed the speech in [men's] mouths and [brought] contention into it." Up to that point, the epic asserts, "the speech of man . . . had been one." The Sumerian version naturally associates the confusion of human language to the Sumerian god. But apart from that, the account is similar to the biblical story. There is no reason to suppose that the biblical author copied the Sumerian account or was even aware of it. What these similarities do suggest, however, is a common understanding of the unity of human languages. The biblical account betrays not only its antiquity but also its authenticity in rendering the views and attitudes of the world it intends to depict.

Note also that the biblical story, like that of its Sumerian counterpart, does not speak of all languages everywhere. Its concern is with "the land" of the Bible—by implication, a common linguistic past with the language of Adam and Eve. The confusion of languages in Genesis 11 has only to do with those languages of the peoples who left off building the city of Babylon.

The Patriarchs

The Biblical Stories About Abraham

Beginning with Genesis 11:27 and continuing through the rest of this book, the Bible recounts the story of one man and his descendants. That man is Abraham, and his descendants are his sons (Isaac and Ishmael), his grandsons (Jacob and Esau), and Jacob's twelve sons.

Abraham was born in the Mesopotamian city of Ur. When he was seventy-five years old, he moved his family and possessions out of Mesopotamia and into the land of Syria-Canaan. There he settled in the central highlands of southern Canaan. Abraham's son Isaac married Rebecca, the daughter of Abraham's brother's son. She was brought to Canaan by Abraham's servant. Isaac and Rebecca had two sons, Jacob and Esau. The biblical narratives are concerned primarily with Jacob, for God had chosen him to be the descendant through whose family a great blessing would come to all humanity. In the course of the biblical narratives, Jacob traveled back to Mesopotamia to find a wife from his mother's family. Because of the trickery of his uncle, Laban, Jacob ended up with two wives, Leah and Rachel.

By the time he returned to Canaan, Jacob had twelve sons. His second youngest, Joseph, was betrayed by his brothers and sold as a slave to Egypt. Through miraculous circumstances, Joseph became a high official in Egypt. Ultimately, because of repeated famine in Canaan, Jacob and his sons took refuge in Egypt, where they enjoyed special status as the family of Joseph.

Documents such as these biblical narratives are notoriously difficult to confirm as historical events. If they appeared in the text as simple fairy tales, we could recognize them as such. But the biblical narratives speak of actual people and places, and they give every indication of being history. They are, moreover, remarkably accurate in the details they give, portraying their characters within a view of the ancient Near Eastern world that we have come to know increasingly well over the last fifty years. The more we learn of the ancient world recounted in the biblical stories, the more authentic these accounts appear.

One must guard against, of course, an overstatement of the case for the historical reliability of these narratives. Not everything in the Bible has by now been proven to be true, but neither has the Bible been proven false by archaeological evidence. There remain, in fact, many facets in the Bible that we will never be able to prove true or false. We will never be able to prove, for example, what Abraham said to his wife Sarah on any given day four thousand years ago. What we can know about the past and about the biblical narratives, however, continues to support the claim of the narratives themselves that these events happened as they are recorded. The primary factor that has led to the widespread acceptance of the historical claims of the biblical narratives has been the precision with which the details of these stories fit historical circumstances in the ancient world.

The Patriarchs and Their World: Part I

The biblical narrative places the events of the lives of Abraham and his descendants in the twenty-first to the nineteenth centuries B.C. In terms of Palestinian archaeology, that puts them within the transition period between the Early Bronze Age and the Middle Bronze Age. From what we know of that period in Canaan, this was a time of transition, and much of the civilized part of the land was in a state of flux. The great empires of old were languishing, and new settlements of people were beginning to appear here and there throughout the land of Canaan.

It is still unclear where the new groups of people came from. Were they immigrants from another part of the ancient world? Or were they indigenous to Syria and Canaan? It was tempting in the past for archaeologists to identify this or that group with the biblical patriarchs. As historical interpretations of these groups of people changed, so did the assessment of the biblical narratives. It was, for example, once thought that these groups of people were engaged in trading and ran caravans throughout the Near East. Many archaeologists thus believed Abraham himself was a "donkey caravaneer." A close look at the biblical text, however, shows clearly that the events in the lives of the patriarchs, with few exceptions, would have laid far out of the reach of a modern archaeologist's spade. One would almost have to discover the actual gravesite of Abraham or Jacob to be able to say anything archaeologically specific about them. Though we are learning more about his world everyday, we still have many questions about how and where Abraham fit into that world.

As it is, we have an abundance of solid archaeological data about the world of the patriarchs. To date, however, no actual remains of any known biblical character from the patriarchal period have come to light. Indeed, we would not expect that to happen. As the Bible itself portrays them, the patriarchs were strangers in a foreign land. They lived as guests in Canaan, moving from site to site as social and economic pressures demanded. Their well-being and status depended on what alliances they could make with the local inhabitants and, sometimes, on their own bare resources. Early on, they did not even own enough land to have a family burial site. They had to purchase a field and burial cave from one of the local inhabitants (Gen. 23).

What we can say of the times in which the patriarchs lived, however, has been aptly put by John Bright, one of the leading historians of that period, "The stories of the patriarchs fit authentically in the milieu of the second millennium ... far better than in that of any later period. The evidence is so massive and many-sided that we cannot begin to review it all" (*A History of Israel*, p. 77).

The Patriarchs and Their World: Part II

There are basically two lines of historical evidence illustrating the patriarchal period. The first looks at the major economic and political factors reflected in the biblical narratives, while the second looks at the social and cultural conditions described in those narratives.

A close look at the biblical narratives reveals both the political and the economic conditions of Abraham's day. (1) The political conditions are reflected in the narrative of Abraham's warfare with the four Eastern kings as recorded in Genesis 14. Both the names of these kings (which are typical second-millennium Near Eastern names) and the type of international alliance they formed in their invasion and subjugation of the Canaanite cities conform with what we know of the history of that period. The Bible clearly suggests that Canaan was not invaded by a single empire at this time, but by a coalition of smaller states. That small detail in the narrative betrays an "insider's" understanding of the political climate of that period. Were that narrative merely made up at a later period, its author would hardly have known to include such historically accurate details.

(2) An interesting economic detail in the biblical narrative also betrays a firsthand knowledge of the actual historical period. When Abraham went down to Egypt, we are told it was because "there was a famine in the land." There are, in fact, wall paintings on Egyptian tombs from this period that show Canaanite visitors in Egypt. We also have a contemporary report of an Egyptian frontier guard that tells of official authorization of Edomites to enter Egypt "to keep them alive and to keep their cattle alive" (Roland De Vaux, *The Early History of Israel*, p. 316). Most recently, using microscopic analysis of soil moisture from ancient ruins in that region, archaeologists, geologists, and soil scientists have determined that the large scale migrations throughout the ancient Near East, of which Abraham was a part, were caused by the onset of a swift and severe drought. That is a remarkable, and unpredictable, confirmation of the historical memory preserved in these early narratives.

The Patriarchs and Their World: Part III

A second line of historical evidence looks beyond the political and economic conditions of the ancient Near East to the social and cultural situations depicted in the biblical narratives. Here too those narratives betray an astute knowledge of the actual conditions of that period as we know it from firsthand historical records and from archaeology. As with the broad political and economic conditions from that period, these historical details would have been virtually impossible for a later writer to fabricate. The fact that the biblical narratives are accurate in such details shows they are based on authentic historical records. What are those details?

It has long been known that the personal names of the patriarchs fit remarkably well with names known to us from historical documents of both Mesopotamia and Egypt. Names such as Abram, Israel, Jacob, and Benjamin were not uncommon, judging from the occurrence of similar names in non-biblical texts. Place-names such as Canaan, Jerusalem, and Meggido are also mentioned outside the Bible.

How could such names be accurately preserved until the time of the writing of Genesis hundreds of years after Abraham and the patriarchs? Knowledge of customs from the early second millennium B.C. also provides an answer to that question. It was not uncommon during that time for individual families to keep remarkably accurate records of the names of their ancestors and key events in their lives. We know, for example, that the early names found in the Assyrian King List (1000 B.C.) were based partly on the private records of minor family chiefs. In some cases, those names can be independently verified and shown to have been accurately preserved over thirteen centuries (Kenneth A. Kitchen, *The Bible in Its World*, p. 66)!

The Patriarchs and Their World: Part IV

Another interesting archaeological detail confirming the biblical narrative's depiction of the lives of the patriarchs is the fact that excavations of places where Abraham lived have shown that these places were occupied only during his lifetime. Places such as the Negev, which in the biblical narratives was frequently visited by Abraham, were not occupied earlier than Abraham's day or for some eight hundred years later.

Furthermore, the freedom with which Abraham moved through the territories of the ancient Near East is a true reflection of the times in which he lived. Such free access to various lands and countries, such as Syria and Egypt, would not have been possible at other periods of time. In Abraham's day, however, social conditions reflected in contemporary nonbiblical texts confirm such freedom of travel and trade. A remarkable painting of "foreign" visitors to Egypt is depicted in a wall painting at the tomb of Khnum-hotep II at Bene Hasan in Lower Egypt. This rare "color photo" of visitors to Egypt gives us a graphic view of what a patriarch may have looked like in the nineteenth century B.C. As clothing and general appearance suggests, people in that day were a tight-knit social group, were well-armed, and traveled with their full families and possessions—just as the biblical naratives depict Abraham and his family.

Other documents from the time of the patriarchs also reveal a deep insight into the social customs of the age of the patriarchs. When we have opportunity to compare details in the biblical narratives with those that have come to light in ancient documents, we often find truly remarkable correspondence. One such detail is the price for which Joseph was sold into slavery in Genesis 37:28. The biblical narrative records that price as twenty shekels of silver. From the laws of the Babylonian king Hammurapi, a contemporary of Joseph, we know that the price of a slave was precisely twenty shekels. At an earlier period, the price was somewhat lower, ten shekels. Later the price increased to forty, fifty, and eventually, 120 shekels (Kenneth A. Kitchen, *The Bible and the Ancient Orient*). It is unlikely that a later writer could have guessed accurately the price of a slave in Joseph's day.

The Patriarchs and Their World: Part V

Artifactual evidence in Palestine. Before Abraham came into the land of Canaan, large cities with fortified walls dotted the horizon. By the time Abraham left his homeland and made his way there, however, those cities had been abandoned and destroyed. The exact reason for this is unknown. Was it an invasion from outside the land? Was it internal strife? We do not know.

In the past scholars usually identified the inhabitants of Canaan in Abraham's day with the "Westerners" or Amorites, who are frequently mentioned in ancient documents from this time period. The changes in Canaan were thus associated with a supposed Amorite "invasion" of Syria and Palestine, and Abraham himself was thought to have been part of such a large-scale migration from Mesopotamia. This view is considered unlikely today because the range of the Amorite migration, as attested in the ancient records, did not extend as far west and south as Canaan. The cultural shift and abandonment of cities in Canaan was thus probably due to typical cultural influences, such as changes in climate and aborted relations with major centers of trade.

What the records show is that when Abraham entered Canaan, it was occupied by shepherds and small farmers, living in tents and eking out a meager existence along the outskirts of the ruins of the former burgeoning cities. Because of the transitional nature of the Canaanite culture at that time, the physical remains of these inhabitants is sparse. That in itself attests to the accuracy of the biblical accounts. In the Genesis narratives, Abraham traverses the land unencumbered by powerful, threatening chieftains. Those whom he meets are shepherds like himself, and they appear to be his equals. He makes alliances with them, and in one case (Gen. 14), defends them against a more powerful outside coalition of four kings from the East. The lack of archaeological evidence for large-scale building and fortifications during this time thus conforms to the biblical picture of Abraham. Had the biblical narratives pictured Abraham coming into contact with huge cities and carefully guarded roadways, the Bible might rightly be charged with historical inaccuracies. It is thus significant that the only real remains of the culture of Abraham's day come from local gravesites, in which we find the implements of everyday life as mentioned in Scripture—weapons, jewelry, tools, and bones.

During the time of the later patriarchs, Isaac and Jacob, however, conditions in Canaan improved sharply. Cities were rebuilt and organized cultures again began to flourish. Such a growing urbanization is also reflected in the biblical narratives. When Abraham visited Shechem, for example, it is called simply "a place" (Gen. 12:6; cf. NKJV). Later, when Jacob returned to Shechem, it is called "a city" (33:18).

The Patriarchs and Their World: Part VI

Inscriptional evidence in Palestine. The cultures surrounding Canaan, particularly Syria, Mesopotamia, and Egypt, had well-developed scribal traditions and a vast literature by the time Abraham entered Canaan. Syria and Mesopotamia utilized a cuneiform script, which consisted of wedges pressed onto a soft clay tablet by a wooden or metal stylus. A certain combination of wedges represented a syllable of a word. Cuneiform texts do not mark the individual letters of a word, but whole syllables. There was thus a need for a great many cuneiform signs (combinations of wedges). Egypt had long used a pictorial script called hieroglyphics for its large monumental texts, and a cursive (handwriting with pen and ink) script with papyrus (an early form of paper). In both Egypt and Mesopotamia, the highly complex systems of writing necessitated learned, professional scribes. Literacy was well out of the range of the average person.

In Canaan, one of the greatest human intellectual developments, the alphabet, was being invented just at the time of the patriarchs. The alphabet simplified writing immensely, taking it largely out of the hands of professional scribes and enabling ordinary people to record their thoughts and actions in writing and in private. Moreover, the alphabet was uniquely designed for use on such easily obtainable writing materials as pottery, leather, wood, and papyrus. Almost anyone who wished to learn to write could do so, and they could write on almost anything.

The alphabet was not a chance discovery. Rather, it developed as the result of deliberate invention. The fact that the Hebrew (Canaanite) alphabet was invented in Canaan at the time the patriarchs were in Canaan has important implications for the biblical narratives. It is often asked whether the patriarchal stories were handed down orally or in writing. Certainly the availability of the alphabet, designed specifically for the Hebrew language, would put written sources for the patriarchal stories well within the range of possibility. One does not need an alphabetic script to speak Hebrew! The alphabet's sole purpose was, and is, writing.

We can go further than that, however. The fact that so much thought was going into the creation and development of the alphabet at the time of the patriarchs suggests that in Canaan there was a great deal of interest and need for just such a simple system of keeping records. The actual success and ultimate triumph of the use of the alphabet in Canaan also suggests not only that it was well received, but that it was well used and widely popular among common people. We know from contemporary records that learned scribal schools, using the old methods of cuneiform did, in fact, exist well into the last centuries of the second millennium B.C.

It thus appears that the popularity and dissemination of the alphabet occurred apart from, and perhaps in opposition to, the official scribal schools. Some of the earliest and more prolific examples of the early Canaanite alphabet are found on the walls of turquoise mines in the southernmost regions of Canaan. Other examples come from short inscriptions on items of everyday life, such as a knife blade and a storage jar. Such examples indicate not only a widespread ability to write, but also a widespread ability to read. Why write on a knife blade unless one assumes others can read it? What all this points to is the high probability that already at the time of the biblical patriarchs alphabetic writing was coming into common use in Canaan.

Why, then, are there so few alphabetic texts in Canaan at the time of the patriarchs? The answer may lie in the fact that the texts would have been written on highly perishable material, such as leather, wood, and papyrus. Though such texts have survived in the arid climate of Egypt, it is unlikely that any such written texts would have survived more than a generation or two in Canaan without being recopied. There is a fragmentary alphabetic text on a potsherd from Gezer that dates from roughly one hundred years after Jacob left Canaan. Because it was written on a piece of pottery, the inscription has survived.

The Patriarchs and Their World: Part VII

Archaeological evidence from Mesopotamia. There are several major archaeological sites of importance to the biblical patriarchs that lie outside the land of Canaan.

Ur. The British excavations of the ancient Sumerian city of Ur early in this century shed much new light on the political and social context of the early life of the patriarchs. Abraham was already quite old when he first walked onto the pages of Scripture. Though it is by no means certain that he came from this Sumerian city of Ur, the general patterns of city life in this Sumerian city was likely characteristic of the "Ur" of his homeland. More recently, several new discoveries have cast additional light on the early "city life" of the earliest patriarch.

Nuzi. The ancient city of Nuzi in northeast Mesopotamia, excavated in the late twenties, has brought to light numerous laws and social customs from the patriarchal period. It was at Nuzi that the people known in the Bible as the "Horites," that is, the Hurrians, had established a major cultural center. Its influence eventually reached throughout the Near East. More recently, the long lost Hurrian city of Urkesh has been identified in northern Syria. This find alone places the influence of Hurrian culture on patriarchal life virtually at the back door of the patriarchs.

Ebla. Another northern Syrian city of great importance to the history of the biblical patriarchs is Ebla, only recently discovered (1975). This city flourished throughout the history of the patriarchs—at times ruling vast regions of Syria, at other times being only a minor segment of other, more powerful kingdoms. Its archives of literally thousands of clay tablets show it to have been a center for business and commerce, as well as a great center of learning. The close similarities between the language of Ebla (Eblaite) and biblical Hebrew are of enormous importance for understanding the history of Hebrew. Many place-names and personal names mentioned in the Bible have been identified in the texts from Ebla. Such information contributes to the ever-increasing knowledge about the life and culture of the biblical patriarchs.

Mari. The ancient city of Mari, located on the west bank of the northern Euphrates River and prominent in the second millennium B.C., was an important city of commerce containing a vast administrative structure. As at Nuzi, Urkesh, and Ebla, thousands of cuneiform texts have also been uncovered from the royal archives of Mari. They too have proven to be a rich source for understanding the legal and social customs of the patriarchal period, not to mention the many geographical and political places of the patriarchal period. Administrative texts from the archives of Mari have also shed much light on ancient trade and commerce.

The Patriarchs and Their World: Part VIII

Archaeological evidence from Egypt. During the early patriarchal period, Egypt was in a general state of disarray (the First Intermediate Period). When Abraham entered Egypt to escape the severe famine conditions of Canaan, the pyramids would have been quite new. By the time he reentered Canaan, however, Egypt had begun to get back on its feet. From the archives and building sites of the vast Middle Kingdom we learn much about conditions in Canaan at the time of the patriarchs.

The Execration Texts (*ANET*, pp. 328–29; *TANE*, pp. 225–26). One of the enduring customs or beliefs of ancient Egypt was the notion that their enemies could be weakened and, indeed, overcome, by the magical use of their names. They thus developed elaborate ceremonies in which clay figurines bearing the names of their enemies were ritually smashed to signify their magical destruction. Many of these figurines, called the "execration texts," contained the names of Egypt's enemies and thus help us understand the general political and social organization of Canaan at that time.

The earliest set of Egypt's execration texts date from about the twentieth century B.C. and are inscribed with some twenty names of towns and regions in ancient Canaan and Syria. They also contain about thirty names of chieftains from the same areas. A close study of these texts reveals a political and social state of affairs in Canaan that closely parallels what is known of that region from the Bible and other artifactual data. Canaan was inhabited by farmers and shepherds who lived in and around small cities and hamlets.

A second set of execrations texts, however, reveals a changing situation in Canaan. In those texts we find the explicit mention of towns and cities known to us from Scripture. These texts clearly indicate that the inhabitants of Canaan were rapidly returning to the kind of developed city life that had earlier characterized that region. Cities were taking the place of tribal groups and alliances. Such a view of Canaan during the time of the patriarchs fits well with the biblical account. When Abraham first passed through Shechem (Gen. 12:6), the biblical text identifies it only as a "place." There Abraham lived in a tent and first built an altar to worship the Lord. Years later, we still find Abraham living in a tent, but we also see him negotiating at "the gate of a city" for a burial site for Sarah (23:10). By the time Jacob returned to Shechem, the biblical narratives have begun to refer to it as a "city" (33:18). He even had to purchase a "plot of ground" in which to pitch his tent (33:19).

The Patriarchs and Their World: Part IX

Further evidence from Egypt. **The Story of Sinuhe** (*ANET*, p. 18; *TANE*, p. 5). This is an ancient autobiographical account of an Egyptian officer, Sinuhe, who was forced to flee from Egypt and travel through Canaan. Sinuhe lived in Canaan many years; he returned to Egypt to die in his own homeland. Since the story dates from the twentieth century B.C., it provides us with an amazingly vivid description of life in Palestine during the time the biblical patriarchs lived there. One can almost imagine Abraham himself as the author of the tale.

As with the other sources of evidence, Canaan was at this time a loosely organized region, largely populated by tribal groups living off their meager farms and flocks. Sinuhe speaks of the abundance of figs, grapes, honey, and olives in that region; "every kind of fruit was on its trees. . . . There was no limit to any kind of cattle." Sinuhe's description sounds remarkably similar to the typical biblical description of Canaan as "a land of wheat and barley, vines and fig trees, pomegranates, olive oil and honey; a land where . . . you will lack nothing" (Deut. 8:8–9).

The Tomb of Khnum-hotep II at Bene Hasan (*TANE*, p. 185). Sinuhe's vivid description of life in Canaan in the patriarchal period is rivaled only by the beautiful color mural of travelers from Canaan, found at the tomb of the Egyptian official Khnum-hotep. Dating from the early nineteenth century B.C., this mural shows a group of thirty-seven "Asiatics" arriving in Egypt from the desert. Its inscription reads, "The arrival, bringing eye-paint, which thirty-seven Asiatics brought to him [Khnum-hotep]."

According to the biblical chronology, Jacob and his sons entered Egypt in the year 1876 B.C. That would have been at the last years of the Middle Kingdom, during the reign of Sesostris III (1878–1841 B.C.), the greatest king of the twelfth dynasty. He is known for his administrative reform that took the political power of that region out of the hands of the local feudal lords (nomarchs) and centralized it into the office of a single administrator, the vizier. Though Joseph is not mentioned anywhere in the Egyptian inscriptions, the administrative achievement during the reign of Sesostris is virtually identical to that of the biblical story of Joseph (Gen. 41:41–57).

There is an interesting papyrus dating from the thirteenth dynasty (1786–1633 B.C.), the time when Israel was in Egypt (*TANE*, ii, p. 87). It lists a number of Semitic servants in the house of an Egyptian official. Many of those listed had become sufficiently assimilated to Egyptian culture to have taken Egyptian names. According to the biblical narratives, Joseph himself took an Egyptian name (Gen. 41:45); the name "Moses" is also Egyptian.

Exodus, the Conquest, and the Judges

Israel in Egypt

The Bible is virtually silent regarding the activities of the Israelites during their four hundred years in Egypt. At the end of Genesis, Israel is a small group of immigrants settling into the delta region of Egypt. They are under the watchful and favorable eye of the pharaoh, and they enjoy the special privileges afforded them as Joseph's family. The book of Exodus, however, opens on the note that the Israelites "were fruitful and multiplied greatly and became exceedingly numerous, so that the land was filled with them" (Ex. 1:7). Moreover, "a new king, who did not know about Joseph, came to power in Egypt" (1:8). This new king viewed the Israelites as a potential threat. He was afraid that in the event of a war, the Israelites might join their enemies and fight against their Egyptian hosts. They might even leave the land and return to Canaan. In an effort to control them, he put the Israelites under "hard labor" and began a full-scale program to limit population growth.

What does archaeology and history reveal about these four hundred silent years? About a century after Jacob entered Egypt a great migration of people from Syria and Palestine, and perhaps even further north, entered Egypt, settling primarily in the delta region of the Nile River. The Egptians called them by the typical expression "rulers of foreign lands"—a term later taken over into Greek and rendered today as the "Hyksos." By 1720 B.C. the Hyksos were strong enough to take control of much of the northern delta region, building their capital city at Avaris. By 1674 B.C. they had overthrown the Egyptian rulers at Memphis and gained control of most of northern Egypt. The Egyptian rulers fled the north and sought refuge in southern Egypt.

Many scholars have tried to associate Joseph and Jacob's sons with the Hyksos kings, especially since both the Hyksos and the Israelites were foreigners living in the northern delta region of Egypt at about the same time. It made sense that the special favor Joseph received could be traced to ethnic ties. Already the Jewish historian Josephus (A.D. 90) believed that the king who elevated Joseph over all Egypt was a Hyksos ruler. The primary problem with such a view is the fact that in 1550 B.C., when the Egyptians were able to defeat the Hyksos and drive them out of the country, they did not seem to bother with the Israelites—though they did make sure that the Israelites did not become involved in any struggle with the Egyptians' enemies. Thus, at least in the Egyptians' mind, the Israelites were not closely linked to the hated Hyksos.

Perhaps the "new king" over Egypt "who did not know about Joseph" was a Hyksos ruler. This would account for their fear that the Israelites would be more numerous than themselves (Ex. 1:9)—an less likely statement on the lips of an Egyptian. Thus when the Egyptians succeeded in riding the land of Hyksos, they continued the suppression of the Israelites that had already been initiated by the Hyksos. Perhaps also the "new king" was the Egyptian king Ahmose, who established the eighteenth dynasty in Egypt by expelling the Hyksos rulers. The measures taken in Exodus 1 to suppress the Israelites may thus have been largely preventative.

Israel and the Exodus

Much debate has centered on the precise date of Israel's exodus from Egypt. There are two possible dates, 1440 B.C. and 1290 B.C. The biblical chronologies, taken at face value, appear to support the earlier date. In 1 Kings 6:1, for example, it is said that Solomon's temple was built 480 years after the Israelites left Egypt and entered the Promised Land. Since we know that Solomon's temple was built in 960 B.C., it is not hard to determine that the Exodus occurred in 1440 B.C. Such a date suggests that Israel left Egypt during the time of the New Kingdom Period, or more specifically, the eighteenth dynasty (1552–1306 B.C.).

Evidence for a later date for the Exodus, however, can also claim biblical support. In Exodus 1:11, for example, we are told that the Egyptian king used Israelite slaves to build the storage cities of Pithom and Raamses. The name Raamses calls to mind the kings of the later nineteenth dynasty in Egypt—thus the Exodus would be much later than 1440 B.C.

We will not attempt to decide this issue. Rather, we will take biblical chronology at face value and draw our comparisons from that perspective. The early date for the Exodus has, in recent years, received a good deal of support, and we may not be entirely wrong with that date.

The most likely candidate for the pharaoh of the Exodus is the eighteenth dynasty king Amenophis II. Are there historical or archaeological indications that during his reign the events of the Exodus occurred? No Egyptian records describe the Exodus. One would not expect such an account. The primary purpose of Egyptian records at that period was to cast the pharaoh in a positive light, and the events of the biblical narratives would do anything but that. There are, however, interesting anomalies in the reign of Amenophis II and his successor, Thutmosis IV, that suggest events such as those recorded in the Bible did, in fact, occur.

The military might of the eighteenth dynasty in Egypt was well known in the ancient world, particularly during the time of Thutmosis III, the predecessor of Amenophis II. Thutmosis' military campaigns in Syria and Canaan (1500–1445 B.C.) are well documented. His first and most important campaign ended with a complete victory over an alliance of Canaanite kings at Megiddo. During his eighth campaign in the year 1460 B.C., Thutmosis III conquered the regions of Syria as far north and east as the Euphrates River. Such exploits show that Egyptian military power was at its height just prior to the time of the Exodus.

In the reign of Amenophis II, Thutmosis' successor, however, Egyptian military power seems to have suffered a considerable setback. This pharaoh launched only two military campaigns in his life. During his reign, Egypt's borders receded from the Euphrates River to well within the confines of the land of Canaan. The significance of such a drastic reversal of military power may well have been the effect of the events of the Exodus, particularly the loss of a large portion of the Egyptian strike force in the waters of the Red Sea.

Another possible indication of the events of the Exodus can be seen in a curious inscription set up in front of the famous Sphinx. In the inscription, Thutmosis IV, the son and successor of Amenophis II, tells of a promise made to him by the Sphinx. In a dream as a young man, the Sphinx promised to give the kingship to Thutmosis IV. What this suggests is that Thutmosis IV did not have a natural claim to the throne; he had to appeal to a divine promise. Perhaps Thutmosis IV was not the heir apparent because of the death of an elder brother. If that were the case, it would accord well with the biblical account of the death of the firstborn son of the pharaoh of the Exodus.

Canaan Before the Time of the Conquest

To gain a full picture of the political conditions in Canaan at the time of the Conquest and settlement, it is necessary to review conditions there before the Israelites arrived. Egyptian records show that the land of Canaan was organized politically into a number of independent territories, each centered around a major city. From about 1700 B.C., these territories were governed by the Hyksos, the same foreign invaders who also gained control over Egypt. Once in Egypt, the Hyksos moved their capital to the northern delta region, to a city they named Avaris. From there they ruled both Egypt and the Canaanite territories. They used a feudal system of apppointed lords and chieftains, who came to represent a sort of military aristocracy.

After the expulsion of the Hyksos, the Canaanite chieftains continued to rule their limited territories until they were subjected to the rule of the Egyptian New Kingdom pharaohs (1570 B.C.). During this period (the eighteenth and nineteenth dynasties), the Egyptians maintained the old territorial and political system that had been laid down by the Hyksos. The local Canaanite city-kings were directly dependent on the pharaoh, who communicated with them by means of dispatches and correspondence.

The Israelite incursion into Canaan, in its initial stages under the leadership of Joshua, fell primarily within the reign of the Egyptian king Amenophis III (1417–1379 B.C.). Although Egypt had ruled Canaan since the expulsion of the Hyksos by Amosis (1570–1546 B.C.), by the time of the Conquest and mainly because of the weakening of Egyptian military might, the local Canaanite chieftains had been left largely to defend themselves against the invading Israelites. Amenophis III's neglect of Egyptian interests in Canaan led to a marked decline of power in those areas.

With the death of Amenophis III, his eldest surviving son, Amenophis IV, assumed the throne (1379–1362 B.C.). This king is famous for the religious revolution he instigated, in which he made the sun god, Re, the sole god of Egypt. The maverick pharaoh also changed his name from Amenophis, which honors the moon god, Amon, to Akhenaton, which honors the sun god, Aton. Some have described this revolution as nothing short of "monotheistic" and have sought to associate his change of heart with the plagues that Moses brought against Egypt. It has long been noted that each of the ten plagues targeted a particular deity in Egypt's pantheon. The goddess of the Nile, for example, was ridiculed when the Nile was turned to blood. The goddess of life, represented as a frog, was also cowed by the heaps of dead frogs stacked along the Nile.

Akenaton also moved his capital city from Thebes, the traditional capital of Egypt, to El-Amarna, an isolated and remote region along the Nile River. During this time the Israelite tribes were separately attempting to take their allotted territories (Judg. 1). An important cache of documents from this period have been uncovered from the ruins of El-Amarna. These documents consist of some 350 baked clay tablets, written by numerous local officials in Canaan and Syria. The importance of these letters lies in the fact that many of them come from the very cities that, at that time, were under attack by the individual Israelite tribes. Some of the letters even mention a group called the "Hapiru," a name similar, if not identical, to the term "Hebrew." These letters may thus provide us with an insiders look at Israel's conquest of Canaan.

Canaan at the Time of the Conquest

The most important feature of the territorial and political organization of Palestine was the city-state—that is, the division of the country into several administrative districts governed by a hereditary prince. The Egyptians left these local princes, or chieftains, in control of their own territories, but they were generally under the close supervision of an Egyptian official. The local princes were responsible for collecting the pharaoh's tribute. If military service was necessary, they had to supply the needed manpower and chariots. In addition to the Egyptian officials, there were also detachments of soldiers garrisoned throughout Canaan, who were to keep the peace.

Archaeological excavation shows a striking contrast between the spacious, well-built houses of the wealthy Egyptian officials and the poorly constructed houses of the common people. The city-states usually owned and controlled the fields surrounding them, as well as a few scattered villages.

Another important feature of the organization of Canaan at this time was the marked political distinction between the hill country and the great valleys. In the valleys and coastal plains of Canaan, the city-states were grouped together closely, with small territorial boundaries. In the southern hill country of Judah, on the other hand, the territories of local city-states were large and enjoyed relative independence from Egyptian rule. The exact political makeup of these cities has not been made clear from ancient documents for the simple reason that they did not maintain close ties with Egypt and hence rarely, if ever, communicated. One reference in the Amarna letters, however, suggests that the southern hill country was governed by a federation of city-states. Such a situation conforms to the biblical account of the covenant Joshua made with the Gibeonites. The "cities" of Gibeon were, in fact, from the southern hill country, and they made a treaty with the Israelites (Josh. 9:15). When the other cities in the region heard about the treaty, they united to attack Gibeon (10:1–5), to punish them for acting independently.

It is interesting to note that in the biblical account, the city of Jerusalem plays a central role in the alliance of cities, which comforms well to the Amarna letters, wherein the king of Jerusalem takes the lead by decrying the havoc brought on the southern hill country by the invading Hapiru. There is also clear evidence in these letters that the central mountain country around Shechem also existed as a large political territory loosely under Egyptian control. This area was governed by an official named Labaya, who seems to have been in control of the entire hill country north of Jerusalem. This is also the area visited by Joshua and the Israelites at the time of the Conquest. According to the Amarna letters, Labaya gave this territory over to the invading Hapiru (the Hebrews?). Note how the biblical account never mentions Joshua's forces having to fight for the territory around Shechem (Josh. 8:30).

The Amarna letters describe a similar situation in the northern region of Galilee. The prince of Hazor broke away from Egyptian rule and attempted to unite northern Canaan under his rule. This accords well with the account of Joshua's battle with an alliance of cities in the north (Josh. 11). Both in the Bible and in the Amarna letters, the king of Hazor was the recognized leader of the Canaanite alliance.

Theories of the Conquest of Canaan

The biblical account of Israel's conquest of Canaan under Joshua is straightforward. After defeating the Moabites and Ammonites east of the Jordan River, the tribes crossed the Jordan and sacked the city of Jericho. They then moved on to conquer the rest of the central, southern, and northern hill county. Late in his life, Joshua allotted territory to each of the tribes. After his death, the tribes, though initially unsuccessful, gained complete control of Canaan and founded the monarchy under David.

Some modern archaeologists have proposed alternative explanations of the process that led to Israel's final settlement in the land of Canaan. Few dispute the general outline of the biblical account—Israel as a people came to occupy Canaan during the Late Bronze Age. That is because already in the late thirteenth century B.C., Egyptian records mention a people called "Israel" occupying the central hill country of Canaan. What is disputed about the Conquest is whether the biblical writers have given us the whole story. Some scholars posit a different explanation of the details of the Conquest. Some have even chosen to drop the word "conquest" altogether in describing Israel's settlement of Canaan.

Peasant revolt theory. A popular recent theory of Israel's settlement in Canaan has asserted that only a few, if any, Israelite tribes ever entered Canaan from the outside. For the most part, it is argued, the Israelites represent a segment of the former peasant population in Canaan, which, under the stress of hard times, fled the local Canaanite cities and established themselves in clans and tribal groups in the remote countryside.

Infiltration theory. Other archaeologists believe the Israelites entered Canaan in stages—gradually finding their places amid the developing city-state cultures. They first took up settlement in the countryside, where they worked as shepherds and farmers. Eventually they gained a foothold in the major cities and, under the leadership of men such as David and Solomon, were able to wrest political control away from the Canaanites and establish their own united monarchy. It is still disputed what proportion of the early Israelites actually infiltrated from outside the land. Many believe they were merely a part of a pastoral fringe of society that had always inhabited the hinterlands of Canaan.

Why are such alternative theories proposed by modern archaeologists? The central question they seek to answer with such theories is why there is so little evidence of a "new population" of people in Canaan during the time they believe Israel entered the land. If Israel invaded Canaan in a large scale military takeover, there should certainly be signs of such a unified struggle in the archaeological remains of the Canaanite cities; but no such signs exist.

What then of the biblical account? Here it is important to note that the Bible does not say that Israel destroyed all the cities they captured. They burned some, such as Jericho and Hazor, but for the most part they took over the cities intact. Though hotly contested among modern archaeologists, it appears that both Jericho and Hazor do, in fact, show signs of destruction at about the time of the biblical conquest (around 1400 B.C.). Moreover, the Israelites are not portrayed in the Bible as a "new population" entering Canaan for the first time. They, in fact, were already Canaanites before they entered Egypt, having lived in southern Canaan for forty years before entering the land from the east. Seen from this perspective, there is little reason to seek an alternative explanation for Israel's settlement of Canaan.

The Period of the Judges I

After the Amarna period (1389–1358 B.C.) we lack inscriptional evidence concerning Palestine for fifty years. With the rise of the nineteenth dynasty, Egypt began again to take an interest in Syria and Canaan. The kings of the nineteenth dynasty set out to restore the former glories of the Egyptian empire, including their influence and holdings in Canaan. To implement their objectives, they moved the capital of Egypt to the old Hyksos city of Zoan, in the northern delta region, renaming it Pa-Ramses (during the reign Ramses II). In a monument set up by Ramses II, the "Stele of the Year 400," the Egyptian king commemorated the four hundredth year of the reign of the Hyksos god Seth. Its intent was apparently to commemorate the establishment of Hyksos rule in Egypt in 1720 B.C.

At the same time as Egypt was seeking to regain its hold on Canaan and Syria, a powerful empire from the north, the Hittite empire, was also seeking to gain influence in the same region. The Egyptians waged many military campaigns in Canaan in an effort to oust the increasingly powerful Hittite influence. One of the results of these struggles for control of Canaan was a series of "treaties" negotiated between the two powers. Those "treaties" have become the object of much attention by biblical scholars. The form of treaty used by the Hittites shows remarkable similarities with the form of the "covenant" God made with Israel at Mount Sinai (see the unit on "Hittite Treaties").

In the first year of his reign, the Egyptian king Seti I waged an extensive military campaign into Canaan. It was his custom to set up victory stelae (monuments) at key sites he conquered. One such stele has been uncovered in Beth-Shean (*ANET*, pp. 253–254; *TANE*, p. 182), on which he boasts of quelling a rebellion of Canaanite kings. In other accounts of his campaigns, Seti mentioned the Israelite tribe of Asher—this is the first extrabiblical notice of that Israelite tribe. In another of Seti's stelae, also discovered at Beth-Shean, we again find the mention of the menacing problem of the Hapiru. According to Seti's account, Egyptian troops were sent to deal with them and soundly defeated them. A possible connection may be drawn between Seti's account of defeating the Hapiru and Judges 1:27, which says that the tribe of Manasseh was unable to take the area around Beth-Shean.

The Period of the Judges II

During the long reign of Ramses II (1304–1237 B.C.), Egypt gained an even greater hold over Syria and Canaan. An interesting papyrus document from this period, called the "Papyrus Anastasi I" (*ANET*, pp. 475–478), gives a narrative account of travel in the lands of Syria and Canaan by an experienced scribe, who recounts many details of life in Canaan during this period. He tells, for example, of the hardships of military campaigns, having to face lions, leopards, and bears, being surrounded by Bedouin "on all sides," crossing over high mountains barefoot, and carrying their chariots on their backs while holding the horses in tow—only to have their provisions stolen by thieves during the night. This is reminiscent of David's having to fight off lions and bears to protect his father's sheep (1 Sam. 17:34).

The scribe at one point boasts of his knowledge of the language of Canaan and begins to write in Hebrew. He mentions a "chief of Asher," one of the tribes of Israel, and tells of an encounter with some local Bedouin "seven to nine feet tall and fierce of face" (cf. Goliath and his brothers in 1 Sam. 17:4; cf. also Num. 13:32–33). "Shuddering seizes thee," the scribe recounts, "(the hair of) thy head stands up, and thy soul lies in thy hand." His pathway, the scribe continues, is "filled with boulders and pebbles, without a toehold for passing by." We know, of course, that in the biblical story of Goliath, David made good use of those "pebbles."

After Ramses II died, Egyptian power and influence in Canaan declined sharply, though his successor, Merneptah (1212–1202 B.C.), did enjoy some military success. In the fifth year of his reign, he defeated a coalition of Lybians and "Sea Peoples," who had come from the Aegean area. This is the first historical record of the wave of new immigrants into the ancient Near East from western regions. It was among these new population groups that the Philistines began their forced entry into Canaan. At about this same time, the Bible tell us that the Israelite judge Shamgar killed a large force of Philistines (Judg. 3:31).

A full-scale battle between the Sea Peoples and the Egyptians took place during the reign of Ramses III (1198–1166 B.C.). In the eighth year of his reign, he fought a major land and sea battle with a group of sea-faring displaced people who had come from the north and were forcing themselves onto Egypt's northern borders. One of the groups was called the "Peleset" (Philistines). The helmets worn by one of the groups matches that of a warrior on an early Mycenaen vase. The Egyptians, however, were able to drive these people back into Canaan, where they settled as Egyptian vassals. In Canaan they occupied the coastal plain and exerted considerable pressure on Israelite settlements.

The Period of the Judges III

The Egyptian king Merneptah reports that on one of his military campaigns, "Israel was laid waste." This is the earliest mention of "Israel" in Egyptian sources—hence the monument on which the inscription is written is called "the Israel Stele." This stele is of particular importance because it speaks of Israel as "a people (settled in the countryside)," rather than living in the central city-states officially sanctioned by the Egyptian government. This has been taken as evidence that Israel was not yet a settled population during Merneptah's reign, implying that the conquest of the land was still in progress in ca. 1210 B.C.

Recently, more background to the Israel Stele has come to light. It has been argued that one of the wall panels at the famous temple in Karnak depicts Merneptah's campaign and the "Israelites" he defeated. In an intriguing piece of detective work, Egyptologist Frank Yurco was able to show that Merneptah's successors had erased his name in the wall panel inscriptions and inserted their own. By carefully removing the later erasures, Yurco demonstrated that the inscriptions were a depiction of Israel and three other Canaanite "enemies" of Egypt. We thus have in these inscriptions a pictorial and written account of Merneptah's battle with the Israelites.

Two features stand out in the Egyptians' depiction of the Israelites. They are dressed in the traditional ankle length clothing of the Canaanites, and they are pictured using chariots in their fight against the Egyptians. Both features suggest an advanced stage of assimilation to Canaanite culture. This supports both the assumption that the Israelites had entered Canaan much earlier than the time of Merneptah, as the Bible appears to suggest, and the notion that the Israelites at this time were virtually indistinguishable from the other inhabitants of Canaan, also suggested by the Bible. The biblical view of Israel during the time of the Conquest is of a people fully urbanized in their culture but who, as a result of divine judgment, had lived for some time in the desert. There is little in the Bible to suggest that the Israelites were not fully capable of moving immediately into the cities and towns of Canaan, places that they did not build but which God delivered into their hands.

Further evidence of the advanced culture of the Israelites at this time is the discovery of a Hebrew "writing exercise tablet" in an Israelite house at Izbet Sartah, a village in central Canaan. The tablet, which dates from the twelfth century B.C., is dramatic proof that the art of reading and writing was now being cultivated among the Israelites.

The Hittite (Suzerainty) Treaty Covenants (1450-1200 B.C.)

When we say that God entered into a covenant relationship with Israel, we understand by this that God initiated a form of action that had its origin in the legal customs of the ancient world. This form of action was the "covenant agreement." In his now classic article in *The Biblical Archaeologist,* George E. Mendenhall of the University of Michigan compared a collection of ancient covenant treaties (Hittite treaties) with the covenant relationship between God and Israel and demonstrated some remarkable similarities.

The significance of these similarities is twofold. (1) They demonstrate the antiquity of the accounts given in the historical books of the Bible in that these accounts show affinities with documents of a known mid-second millennium B.C. date. (2) They help illumine the theological significance of Israel's covenant with God—namely, that Yahweh, the Sovereign King, having graciously brought Israel out of Egypt, entered into a relationship with them in which Israel agreed to obey the rules and regulations of the agreement. Recognition of Yahweh as King and Israel as obedient subjects (vassals) henceforth became the dominate theme in Israel's history and theology (cf. Judg. 8:23).

The primary purpose of the suzerainty treaty was to establish a firm relationship of mutual support between two parties, in which the interest of the Hittite king was of primary concern. Although a two-way relationship was established, stipulations were given that were binding only on the vassal—only the vassal took the oath of obedience. Although the treaties frequently contained promises of help and support to the vassal by the king, there was no legal formality by which the Hittite king bound himself to any specific obligation. Thus, since the Hittite king was free of any obligation to the vassal, the vassal's only recourse was to trust in the goodwill of the king. The obligations (stipulations) imposed on the vassal were called "the words" of the sovereign.

The Covenant Form of the Suzerainty Treaty

The Hittite suzerainty treaties all bore a specific form that the kings used when they drafted them. Here are its elements:

1. Preamble: "Thus (says) [Personal Name], the great king...."
   This identifies the author of the covenant, the Hittite suzerain.
2. Historical prologue
   a. This section describes in detail the previous relations between the two parties—the great king and the vassal.
   b. This section emphasizes the benevolent deeds that the Hittite king has performed for the benefit of the vassal.
   c. The historical prologue is an essential ingredient of the suzerainty treaty. "What the description amounts to is this, that the vassal is obligated to perpetual gratitude toward the great king because of the benevolence, consideration, and favor that he has already received. Immediately following this, the devotion of the vassal to the great king is expressed as a logical consequence" (Korosec, *B. Hethitische Staatsvertraege,* Leipzig, 1931).
3. Stipulations
   a. This section details the obligations imposed on and accepted by the vassal.
   b. The Hittite stipulations include:
      • Prohibition of any other foreign relationship.
      • Prohibition of any enmity against anyone under sovereignty of the great king.
      • The vassal must answer any call to arms sent by the king. To fail to respond is a breach of covenant.
      • The vassal must hold lasting and unlimited trust in the great king.
      • The vassal must appear before the king once a year.
      • Controversies between vassals are unconditionally to be submitted to the king for judgment.
4. Provision for deposit in the temple and periodic public reading
   a. This provision is intended to ensure continual familiarity of the entire populace with the obligations of the treaty.
   b. Such a reading will increase the respect for the great king by recounting his benevolent deeds for his vassals.
5. List of witnesses
6. The curses and blessings formula

a. Although it was surely understood that the king (Hittite) would use military power to punish any breach of the treaty, there is no mention of such a threat in the treaty.

b. The consequences of obeying or disobeying the stipulations of the treaty are expressed only in terms of "blessings" and "curses."

7. A formal oath ceremony

Although this section of the treaty-making process is not written and thus has not survived, there certainly existed a formal ceremony by which the vassal pledged his obedience to the Hittite king (suzerain).

Covenant Forms in Israel

The Mosaic covenant shows important similarities to the type of treaties used by the Hittites with their vassals. This is not to say that God used a "Hittite treaty" to establish his relationship with Israel. It is only to say that certain features of the covenant treaties of the ancient world lent themselves to the full expression of Yahweh's relationship to Israel. These features are shared by the Hittite treaties because they were apparently common in the international relations during the second millennium B.C.

Not only is the covenant form noticeable in Exodus 19-24, it can also be seen in the book of Deuteronomy. In fact, the entire structure of this book appears to follow the covenant-treaty form. Since part of the stipulation of the covenant treaty was the periodic public reading of the treaty document, these documents were frequently updated or "renewed" in a formal ceremony. Many features of the book of Deuteronomy suggest that it may have been written as a document for such an occasion.

1. Preamble (Deut. 1:1-5)
2. Historical prologue (Deut. 1:6-4:49)
3. Two large stipulation sections are found in chapters 5–26:
   a. Chapters 5–11 present the covenant way of life in more general and comprehensive terms.
   b. Chapters 12–26 add more specific requirements to the covenant way of life.
4. Curses and blessings (Deut. 27–30)
5. Provisions of continual maintenance of the covenant (Deut. 31–34)

   Included in this section are two elements of the vassal treaty form:

   a. Calling of witnesses to attest to the covenant (chs. 32–33).
   b. Provision for periodic public reading of the covenant (31:9–13)

The United Monarchy

The Period of Saul, Israel's First King

The Egyptian story of Wen-Amun (*ANET*, pp. 25–29), which dates from the beginning of the eleventh century B.C., provides an eyewitness account of conditions in Canaan at the end of the time of the judges. The story tells in picturesque narrative the tale of an Egyptian official, Wen-Amun, sent to the northern Canaanite city of Byblos to purchase wood. The official meets trouble nearly every step of his journey. There are thieves and crooked officials on all sides. As he himself puts it, "injustice is done in every town." Those words are remarkably similar to the description of Canaan at this time in Judges. 21:25: "In those days Israel had no king; everyone did as he saw fit." We also learn in 1 Kings 5–7 that King Solomon sent officials to the same region to acquire building materials for the temple in Jerusalem.

The impression gained in reading Wen-Amun's account of Canaan is that it was relatively free of Egyptian influence. The local officials he meets are free to exert their own influence, sometimes quite arbitrarily. The Philistines had settled the seacoast towns of Ashkelon, Ashdod, and Jaffa. Wen-Amun visited the town of Dor along the northern coastline of Canaan, where he met a prince named Beder and his people, the Tjeker, who were part of the groups of "sea peoples" who had attempted to force themselves into Egypt one or two centuries earlier.

The Philistines at this time were organized into a confederation of cities, each ruled by a prince. They controlled much of the coastline of Canaan and extended their rule inland as far as the Jezreel Valley and the northern Transjordan region. For that reason we hear much about them in the books of Samuel. The Philistines were powerful, largely because of their monopoly on iron tools and weapons. They themselves had imported iron into Canaan from Asia Minor, but were careful not to let the Israelites gain access to such a potentially lethal material. As the writer of 1 Samuel says, "Not a blacksmith could be found in the whole land of Israel, because the Philistines had said, 'Otherwise the Hebrews will make swords or spears!'" (1 Sam. 13:19).

According to 1 Samuel 4, the fall of the Israelite town of Shiloh in mid-eleventh century B.C. represented a major victory for the Philistines. Archaeological excavations at Shiloh suggest that it was, in fact, destroyed by fire at this time. With its fall and the consequent ascendancy of the Philistines in Israelite territory, the Philistine army maintained foot soldiers and equipment at strategically important sites. Saul's death marked the final stage in the Philistine hegemony in Israel. They now controlled all of north and central Palestine west of the Jordan River. The name "Palestine," in fact, stems from the fact that the "Philistines" once held this territory.

Saul, the first king of Israel, thus ruled during the time when the Philistines were pressing hard on Israel's western borders. One of his central tasks was to defend Israel against this threat. He was, in effect, a permanent judge, providing little, if any, political organization to his kingdom. He built his home in the city of Gibeah, situated on a high hill three miles north of Jerusalem. Excavations at Gibeah have uncovered a large rectangular enclosure, used mainly for defensive purposes. Its walls were made of rough hewn blocks of stone. At each of their corners was placed a high tower. Within this citadel were found many bronze arrowheads and slingstones—common weapons from that period. The entire enclosure was destroyed by fire during the time of Saul.

David and Goliath

David is the central figure in the history of Israel. He united the Israelites into their first real monarchy, established Israel's military supremacy over the troublesome Philistines, and extended Israel's territorial holdings far into adjacent countries. During his reign, Israel became an empire.

David's own beginnings, like that of the nation itself, lay in tending herds in the remote countryside. His first encounter with national issues that led down the road to the kingship was his show of courage against the Philistine giant, Goliath. Judging from his name, Goliath was a recent immigrant from western Asia Minor. Both the kind of warfare he was trained for and the type of armor he wore (fitting the descriptions of Aegean warriors in early Greek literature) suggest a western Asia Minor context. It was common in the wars of the Aegeans to influence the outcome of a battle by having two champions engage in a preliminary dual (cf. also 2 Sam. 2:14).

An interesting example of such a dual is found in the Egyptian *Tale of Sinuhe* (twentieth century B.C.). In his travels through Canaan, the Egyptian official Sinuhe was forced to dual with a local Canaanite (Retenu) hero. Sinuhe says, "A mighty man of Retenu came, that he might challenge me in my own camp. He was a hero without his peer, and he had repelled all of [Retenu]." The next day, Sinuhe continues, the whole countryside had come to see the dual. The Canaanite hero met him in camp. He attacked, but Sinuhe dodged his arrows and javelins. When the hero charged at him, Sinuhe says, "I shot him and my arrow stuck in his neck. He cried out and fell on his nose. I felled him with his (own) battle-axe." At that Sinuhe plundered the house and belongings of the local Canaanite chieftain who had been responsible for the dual. The similarities with David's battle with Goliath are transparent.

The biblical writer makes special mention of Goliath's spear, which had an iron tip—an innovative weapon in Canaan at that time. The shaft of Goliath's spear "was like a weaver's rod" (1 Sam. 17:7). The characteristic feature of a weaver's rod at that time was the row of loops attached to it to guide the beam along the warp (threads). In a similar fashion, Aegean warriors carried spears with loops attached to them, which served as a kind of sling for throwing the spear. By slinging the spear as it was thrown, the shaft was given additional rotation and hence traveled a greater distance.

David's use of a sling was also a common weapon at this time. The sling had proven to be an accurate and deadly instrument. According to Judges 20:16, there were seven hundred left-handed Benjamites who "could sling a stone at a hair and not miss." Wall panels from Nineveh contain numerous carvings of battle scenes in which "slingmen" formed a regular unit of the fighting force. The sling had the greatest distance of any ancient weapon.

The location of David's dual with Goliath was the Valley of Elath. That valley guarded the only convenient access to Hebron, Bethlehem, and the Judean hillside. It was thus of great strategic importance that the Philistines be held in check at Elath. Saul waged an effective campaign against the Philistines, but was unable to stem the tide. Ultimately he died fighting the Philistines in defense of his country (1 Sam. 31:4).

David's Kingdom

As late as 1992 it was still possible to say that no extrabiblical inscription had ever been found containing a reference to David. This is, however, no longer true. In the summer of 1993 an American archaeologist, Dr. Avraham Biran, uncovered in the ancient city of Dan a fragment of a stone monument with the name "David" inscribed on it. The inscription, which dates from about 850 B.C., is in Aramaic and contains thirteen lines of text referring to the "house of David." The inscription was likely a victory stele set up in the Israelite city of Dan by the king of Damascus, commemorating his defeat of several northern Israelite cities. According to Biran, the "king of Israel" mentioned in the inscription was probably Baasha and the king of the "house of David" was Asa. The mention of the "house of David" is of phenomenal importance as it makes certain what had always been assumed, that David founded the monarchy in the south kingdom of Judah.

Through his various military conquests, David established a considerable empire. In the Transjordan region, the states of Moab, Edom, and Ammon were under his control (cf. 2 Sam. 8:2, 14; 12:30). On his western borders, David subdued the Philistines (5:17–25), and to the north and northeast he extended his rule over the Arameans nearly as far as the Euphrates River (8:3–11). When Solomon succeeded his father to the throne, he inherited this vast empire and took upon himself the task of its administration.

David and Jerusalem

Few artifacts remain from the time of David. His kingship was marked by warfare and military expansion. He apparently spent little time on building projects. David and his army captured the city of Jerusalem from the Jebusites. This city had changed hands several times since the time of the Conquest (cf. Judg. 1:8,21), but was never fully established as an Israelite city. Much of the area of Jerusalem in David's time lay to the south of the present city, on a small point called the "Ophel" (or "hill"). During Roman times, the hill was used as a quarry; consequently, a good deal of what had remained of the earlier city has long been removed.

According to 2 Samuel 5:11, the king of Tyre sent craftsmen to Jerusalem to build a house for David. There is no trace of that house today. There are, however, remains of a wall built around the early city of Jerusalem by its former occupants, the Jebusites. Just outside the wall is a spring of water called the Gihon. The wall was built far enough down the slope of the hill to provide access to the spring, which was gained by means of an underground shaft tunneled through solid rock. During a siege on the city, water could be drawn from the spring from within the city wall. When he captured the city, David no doubt strengthened the wall around the ancient city of Jerusalem and built further fortifications.

In making plans to capture Jerusalem, David issued the order that "anyone who conquers the Jebusites will have to use the water shaft" (2 Sam. 5:8). Many believe this text records a clever stratagem of David that enabled him to capture the city whereas others before him had failed. David knew of the "water shaft" that led from the spring of Gihon to inside the city walls. He thus sent a detachment of soldiers through the shaft and into the city. Having captured the city, David made it his capital, Zion.

Inside the ancient wall of Jerusalem archaeologists have uncovered a massive foundational structure of piled rocks that many believe to be the base of David's house and fortress. Some have identified this structure with the "millo," or acropolis, that David built (2 Sam. 5:9). The Hebrew word *millo* means simply "filled (with stones)" and thus fits what the archaeologists' have found. Since the "millo" continued to be repaired by subsequent Judean kings, it is likely that David's buildings were removed and replaced by others.

Solomon's Kingdom

David's son and successor, Solomon, sought to maintain good relationships with the nations around him by entering a series of trade agreements. Many of his foreign wives (1 Kings 11:1–3) were probably the result of such alliances. For example, "Solomon made an alliance with Pharaoh king of Egypt and married his daughter. He brought her to the City of David" (3:1). It was crucial for Solomon's caravan trade with Arabia to the south that he maintain the control over Edom that his father David had initiated (2 Sam. 8:13–14). The Edomites were also the key to maintaining Solomon's sea trade routes through the port at Ezion Geber. Solomon maintained a fleet of merchant ships in the Red Sea, which made regular trips carrying gold, silver, and rare products from Ophir (possibly modern Somalia) to Solomon's ports on the Red Sea. But during Solomon's reign, the control of key cities such as Damascus was beginning to slip out of his grasp. The Aramaic king, Rezon son of Eliada, rebelled against Solomon's rule in Damascus and established himself there as king (1 Kings 11:23–25).

Solomon's most important alliance was with Tyre (1 Kings 5:1–12). Tyre was a Phoenician city, established (or reestablished) in the twelfth century B.C.—the capital city for the entire region. Its chief leader was Hiram I. Solomon agreed to supply wheat and olive oil in exchange for lumber and building supplies from Lebanon.

Hiram also sent craftsmen to help with Solomon's building projects. Examples of the work of Phoenician artisans are known from several sites outside Canaan. Many of their carved wood and ivory pieces betray a strong influence of Egyptian style. Unfortunately, little of their work is known from excavations either in their own land or in Israel. Thus we can only guess what styles they may have chosen, or would have been permitted, in decorating Solomon's buildings.

Modern textbooks have usually viewed Solomon's temple in light of what appear to have been similar temple models in the ancient Near East. An eighth-century B.C. royal palace at Tell Tainat in northern Syria, for example, has a temple attached to it that resembles the biblical description of Solomon's temple in certain key elements. It had three main rooms: a porch with two columns, a main hall, and an inner room. But we do not know anything for certain about the decorative style used by the craftsmen. What did the "cherubim" look like? How were they depicted in Solomon's temple? What motifs were employed in carving the "palm trees and open flowers" on the walls? To what extent were the Phoenician artisans left to their own designs? Was there a characteristic "Israelite" style of art? Did the prohibitions of images in God's law have an impact on the artistic styles and motifs that Solomon would have approved?

Solomon's Domestic Policies

Because of his massive building projects, much has survived from Solomon's time. His successful foreign policy resulted in a flourishing economy. Under Solomon's leadership, Israel became "urbanized." For the most part, what could be gained from foreign trade belonged solely to the king himself. During Solomon's reign, many cities throughout his kingdom greatly expanded beyond their old walls. The introduction of the iron-tipped plow increased agricultural productivity.

Solomon's reign also saw marked cultural development. In 1908 a small limestone tablet with Hebrew inscribed on it was discovered at Gezer. The tablet, now called the Gezer Calendar, dates to this era (tenth century B.C.). The text, written in biblical Hebrew, is a short poem that recounts the seasons of the year. It was probably a school child's practice tablet and hence witnesses to widespread literacy. The biblical narratives themselves speak of Solomon's official records and his care for the administration of his government (cf. 1 Kings 11:41).

Several books of the Bible also suggest that this was an important period for the composition and preservation of Scripture. The composition of the book of Samuel possibly dates from this time, as does the collecting of many of the psalms of David (cf. the document entitled "The Prayers of David" in Ps. 72:20). Solomon himself, according to many passages in Scripture, was the author of much of the wisdom literature in the Bible (e.g., Prov. 1:1).

As the cities of Israel began to grow and taxation became an increasingly important source of revenue, the need arose for a stronger internal administrative structure. According to 1 Kings 4:7–19, Solomon established a twelve-district administrative system. Each district was to provide for the affairs of the royal house for one month of the year. Historians have pointed to the fact that these administrative districts often cut across traditional tribal boundaries and thus may well have caused internal tensions. Such tensions probably played a part in the division of the kingdom after Solomon's death (cf. 12:4).

Solomon also established fortified royal cities throughout his kingdom (1 Kings 9:15–19): Jerusalem (central), Hazor (north), Megiddo (northwest), Gezer (southwest), and Tamar (south). He built these cities with "forced labor" (9:15). They guarded major thoroughfares and regions and were arranged strategically throughout the land so that his forces could respond quickly to trouble anywhere. These cities may also be linked to the "chariot cities" that Solomon also built (10:26). At Megiddo archaeologists have uncovered what appear to be "store houses." In the past these were interpreted as "stables" from the time of Solomon and hence identified as places where his chariot forces were garrisoned. Today that interpretation has been largely discarded. Moreover, these structures probably date from a later period.

The Divided Kingdom (Israel)

Jeroboam and the Division of the Kingdom

Already during the reign of Solomon rebellion broke out, led by Jeroboam son of Nebat, an Ephraimite (1 Kings 11:26). He had been made chief of the forced labor and was encouraged in his rebellion by the prophet Ahijah from Shiloh (11:29). Ahijah told Jeroboam that the Lord had chosen him to be king of the ten tribes of northern Israel. When news began to spread of his rebellion, Solomon moved quickly and Jeroboam fled to Egypt, seeking the protection of the Egyptian king Shishak.

After Solomon's death, his son Rehoboam was unable to hold the kingdom together. The northern tribes rejected Rehoboam's attempts at harsh rule and called Jeroboam out of exile, who then became king of the northern federation of tribes. The once glorious empire of David was reduced to the tiny kingdom of Judah. The Arameans to the north of Israel quickly broke ranks with what was left of Solomon's kingdom. To the southwest, the Philistine cities regained their independence. Ammon to the east not only broke free of Israelite control, but also, with Moab, quickly became a serious threat to Judah's eastern border.

Such events had disastrous economic effects on the already weakened kingdoms of Israel and Judah, along with irreversible religious consequences. The northern kingdom of Israel, afraid of losing the allegiance of the people, forsook the Lord through Jeroboam's leadership and charted a completely new form of religious life. The king refused to allow his countrymen to travel to Jerusalem to participate in the worship of God at the temple. Instead, he established his own temples in two of his cities: Bethel on his southern border and Dan to the north. At each of these temples, he set up images of golden calves.

It is not certain what Jeroboam meant to represent by these golden calves. They were certainly a reflection, and perhaps imitation, of the golden calf that Israel made at the foot of Mount Sinai (Ex. 32). Some historians suggest that Jeroboam was trying to unite a wide variety of ancient beliefs in his new religion, including features of Canaanite worship. The bull was a well-known feature of Canaanite mythology. The Canaanite deity Baal was often called simply "the bull." Others have argued that the calves were not objects of worship, but rather were pedestals on which the deity sat or rode. In any case, the biblical writers viewed the calves as "other gods" (1 Kings 14:9). Recent excavations have recovered a small (about twelve inches high) cultic figurine of a bull, overlaid with gold.

Jeroboam thus succeeded in establishing a rival worship in the northern kingdom. That worship was sorely attacked by those prophets who spoke on behalf of the God of the Bible (1 Kings 13). A central theme running through most of the book of Kings is that Jeroboam's false worship centers ultimately led to the downfall of the northern kingdom.

The Dynasty of Omri

The dynasty of Jeroboam lasted only two years after his death. His son Nadab was assassinated by a rival named Baasha (1 Kings 15:27). Baasha retained control of the throne during his lifetime; but his son Elah was killed only two years after becoming king (15:21, 33; 16:6) by one of his own military commanders, Zimri, who in turn reigned only one week (16:15). When the general populace heard of his conspiracy against Elah, they appointed an army captain, Omri, as king and set out to capture Zimri in his own capital city of Tirzah. In utter desperation, Zimri burned down his own royal palace and himself in it, rather than surrender to Omri's forces. Omri then occupied the city and began to rebuild it. There is archaeological evidence of extensive destruction at the site of this ancient city during this period. There are also several partially completed buildings at the city, apparently abandoned when Omri moved to his new capital to Samaria.

Omri presided over a stable and powerful kingdom. The Bible has little to say about his reign, though much is written about the reign of his son Ahab. Viewed from a political and economic point of view, Omri was one of Israel's most powerful rulers. Long after his dynasty had been wiped out, the kingdom of Israel was still known as "the house of Omri."

Archaeological evidence suggests that Israel regained much of its former glory under the kings who ruled from the dynasty of Omri. During this time the new capital of the northern kingdom, Samaria, was selected and built. Omri had purchased the site of this city with his own wealth (1 Kings 16:24). It was thus a royal city, belonging to the house of Omri, much like Jerusalem belonged to the house of David. Also like Jerusalem, Samaria was well situated on a high hill and thus easily defended. Both Omri and his son Ahab undertook extensive building projects there, which are noted even today for their superior technical features as well as their beauty. The royal palace was trimmed with intricately carved pieces of ivory.

Other cities in the northern kingdom were also rebuilt and fortified during the dynasty of Omri. Hazor in the north became a major storage city for the northern sector of the kingdom. Remains of large storage facilities are still found there today. Of particular interest is the fact that private homes excavated at Hazor from this period give abundant evidence of a high degree of literacy. Written texts inscribed on pieces of broken pottery (ostraca) suggest that writing was a part of the everyday life of common people. Most of the texts deal with ordinary business transactions, recording the receipt of produce (such as wine and oil). Though difficult to date (the dating of such texts is based on the style of the handwriting and the strata in which the texts are uncovered), the texts are usually assigned to the period after the reign of Ahab.

Writing materials such as papyrus and stone were more expensive and reserved for the professional scribes.

One of the most startling texts from this early period of Israelite history is the Moabite Stone (see next unit).

The Moabite Stone

The ancient land of Moab lay just to the southeast of the kingdom of Israel. The Bible traces their lineage back to the time of Abraham (Gen. 19:37). The first mention of the Moabites outside the Bible is found in the inscriptions of the Egyptian king Rameses II in the late thirteenth century B.C. This nation was deeply troubled by Israel's conquest of Canaan during the time of Moses and Joshua and went to great lengths to thwart Israel's advance into the land. On one occasion they hired a renown seer, Balaam, to cast a spell over Israel and thus halt their entry into land that the Moabites had themselves, apparently, set their eyes on. The Lord, however, permitted Balaam only the option of blessing Israel, thus reversing the strategy of Moab. In a further act of humiliation, the Lord gave to Balaam a prophecy of the coming of a future king in Israel who would subdue the people of Moab and bring them into his kingdom (Num. 24:17–19). Eventually, David brought the Moabites under his rule (2 Sam. 8:2).

As the Israelites were preparing to enter Canaan, the Moabites sent their women into the Israelite camps and invited them to disobey the Lord by participating in sexually immoral religious celebrations (Num. 25:1–3). During Israel's early occupation of Canaan, the Moabite king Eglon reeked considerable havoc on many of the Israelite tribes (Judg. 3:12–30). In other words, a considerable animosity was building between Israel and Moab.

David's conquering of Moab temporarily settled the issue, but during the early years of the divided kingdom, Israel's grip on the kingdom of Moab began to loosen. Though the Bible does not mention it, the powerful Israelite king Omri reasserted control over the Moabites, but not without engendering further hatred. During the time of Ahab or later, Moab fought for and gained their independence. The Israelite king Jehoram later tried to regain Moab, but it was too much for the politically and religiously weakened Israel. Moab remained bitter enemies of Israel and assisted the Babylonians in their final destruction of the southern kingdom (2 Kings 24:2).

The Moabite Stone, a remarkable document from the days of the ancient Moabite king Mesha, was discovered over a hundred years ago. This lengthy inscription boasts of Mesha's gaining independence from Israelite rule. It is, in effect, the other side of the story of the Bible. The inscription continues to supply valuable insights and information about the days of the divided monarchy in Israel (see *ANET*, p. 320).

The inscription, probably intended as an inscription for a Moabite temple, begins with the king introducing himself as "Mesha, the son of Kemosh[-yatti], the king of Moab," and proceeds to praise the Moabite god Kemosh for giving Mesha victory over his enemies. He then turns to recount the history of Moab's sad past under Israelite dominance and their present glories as an independent state. Mesha speaks about Omri, the king of Israel, who "oppressed Moab for many days," and of his son (Ahab), who continued that oppression. During the reigns of Omri's son and his successors, however, Mesha insists, the tables were turned. "I have triumphed over him [Ahab]," boasts Mesha, "Israel has perished forever." Though we know from subsequent history that Mesha's statement is an exaggeration, the Bible does confirm that after Ahab's death, Mesha rebelled against the northern kingdom and won independence (2 Kings 1:1; 3:4–5).

Elijah and Elisha

It has long been recognized that the account of Elijah and Elisha depicts a clash between the prophets of Yahweh and Queen Jezebel, who propagated the worship of Baal in Israel. But until recently, little was known regarding the details of this confrontation because we knew little about the religious ideas of Baal worship in ancient Canaan.

In 1929 a cache of clay tablets was discovered at Ras Shamra, the ancient city of Ugarit, on the northern coast of the Mediterranean Sea. Written in a language similar to biblical Hebrew, these texts contain religious mythologies, employing several motifs and recurring themes extolling the works of the Canaanite god Baal. They have provided a rich source of historical background to the conflicts that raged between the prophets Elijah and Elisha and Jezebel's prophets of Baal. Elijah and Elisha were well acquainted with the Baal mythologies that circulated in ancient Canaan. At least four religious motifs are found both in the Ugaritic myths and in the biblical accounts of Elijah and Elisha.

(1) *The fire motif.* The Ugaritic texts indicate the belief that Baal controlled fire and lightning. In an carved image of Baal also found at Ugarit, the god is shown holding a club in one hand and a stylized bolt of lightning in the other. Baal is described as the one who "flashed lightning to the earth." Given this picture of Baal in Canaanite mythology, Elijah's use of fire to test Baal and demonstrate that the Lord alone is God (1 Kings 18:24; 2 Kings 1:10–12) seems remarkably appropriate.

(2) *The rain motif.* Canaanite mythology also ascribed to Baal the power of making the land fertile by sending rain. The club in the image of Baal mentioned above was intended to symbolize his supremacy over thunder and the forces of rain. Arising out of the bolt of lightning is a plant of some kind, symbolizing the vegetation that comes from his sending rain. One Ugaritic text reads: "The heavens rain oil, the wadies run with honey, so I know the mighty one, Baal, lives. Lo, the prince, lord of the earth, exists." Several events in the stories of Elijah and Elisha specifically show that God alone has power over rain and vegetation. Elijah began his ministry by proclaiming to the Israelites: "As the LORD, the God of Israel, lives, . . . there will be neither dew nor rain in the next few years except at my word" (1 Kings 17:1).

(3) *The oil and corn motif.* The Ugaritic texts clearly indicate that Baal is master over the forces of vegetation and fertility. One of his frequent titles is "son of Dagon"—the vegetation god of the ancient Semitic people. Frequent episodes in the Elijah and Elisha narratives show that God alone has power over the plants and productivity of the land. Elijah was fed miraculously by ravens, who brought him bread and meat (1 Kings 17:6). The widow's bowl of flour and jar of oil in Zarephath would not be exhausted "until the day the LORD gives rain" (17:14).

(4) *The river motif.* All mythologies in the ancient Near East contain descriptions of the struggles between gods. Baal also has his rivals, the most serious of which is the river god, Judge River, or Prince Sea. The Ugaritic texts emphasize Baal's control over the river. With the help of a special stick, Baal crushes the head of the River. The biblical narratives also show how both Elijah and Elisha, the prophets of God, were given power to split the Jordan River. They, of course, did not need to resort to magic; they simply prayed to God, and God answered.

The Rise of Assyria and Fall of Israel

The nation of Assyria played a central role in the history of Israel and Judah during the monarchial period. So important was its influence on the internal affairs of all the nations in Syria and Canaan that the prophet Isaiah refers to it as "the rod of [the LORD's] anger" (Isa. 10:5).

The first great Assyrian leader was Tiglath-Pileser III (745–727 B.C.), known as Pul in the Old Testament (2 Kings 15:19). With his reign, Assyria became the undisputed power through most of the ancient Near East. Beginning in 743 B.C., Tiglath-Pileser III led several military campaigns into Syria. By 738 he had gained control over most of the Syrian states. Under him, Assyria adopted the policy of relocating rebellious subjects to distant countries and repopulating their lands with subservient peoples. That policy ultimately led to the deportation of the northern kingdom of Israel. The Israelite king Menahem (745–738 B.C.) was the first king of the northern kingdom to pay tribute to Tiglath-Pileser III (2 Kings 15:19). In one of his own building inscriptions from his palace in Calah, this Assyrian king makes note of the tribute he enforced on "Menahem of Samaria" (*ANET*, p. 283). The payment of such a tribute almost certainly meant that Menahem had surrendered to Tiglath-Pileser III's rule.

In the turbulent years that followed Menahem's reign, an officer of his court, Pekah, assassinated Menahem's son and successor, Pekahiah, and assumed the throne. Soon afterward, Pekah joined with the Aramean king Rezin to mount an opposition to Assyrian rule in Syria and Palestine. Both Pekah and Rezin attempted to force Judah to join in their rebellion, but the Judean king, Jotham, refused (2 Kings 15:37). During the reign of Jotham's successor, Ahaz, Pekah and Rezin besieged Jerusalem and attempted to replace Ahaz with one of their own allies. Ahaz appealed to Tiglath-Pileser III for help (16:7; cf. Isa. 7:1–8:18) and thereby incurred the wrath of the prophet Isaiah.

Tiglath-Pileser III responsded to Ahaz's appeal by launching a devastating attack on Syria and Israel. Pekah was removed from the throne, and the pro-Assyria Hoshea replaced him. An account of this series of events is recorded not only in 2 Kings 15:30, but also in Tiglath-Pileser III's own annals: "Israel and all its inhabitants and their possessions I led to Assyria. They overthrew their king Pekah and I placed Hoshea as king over them" (*ANET*, p. 284). Hoshea reigned as a loyal vassal of Tiglath-Pileser III and continued to pay tribute to his successor, Shalmaneser V. But sensing a moment of weakness in Assyrian control over Israel, Hoshea broke off payment of tribute to Shalmaneser V and appealed for help from Egypt.

Egypt proved to be of little help, however. Shalmaneser V besieged Samaria for three years. In the ninth year of Hoshea's reign (722 B.C.), the

Assyrian forces captured Samaria and carried the northern kingdom off into exile. That was the end of Israel as an independent people. The biblical narratives say only that the city was captured and taken into exile by "the king of Assyria" (2 Kings 17:6). The context suggests it was Shalmaneser V, though he died in that same year and his son and successor, Sargon II, claims in his annals to have captured Samaria (*ANET*, p. 284). Most historians believe, however, that Sargon II's records merely take credit for what his father had accomplished before his death.

The Divided Kingdom (Judah)

The Archaeology of Jerusalem

After the death of Solomon, his kingdom was divided. The kings of the house of David continued to rule in Jerusalem over what came to be called the kingdom of Judah.

Archaeological excavations of the southern kingdom have been extensive in this century, but they have also been hampered by the fact that much of the region is presently occupied by modern cities and towns. It is sometimes impossible to excavate a site that is presently occupied. Many modern homes and businesses in Jerusalem, for example, are situated on important archaeological sites. Arguably the most important site in all of ancient Palestine, the Jerusalem temple, has, since A.D. 691, been the site of the Islamic Dome of the Rock.

In spite of such difficulties, excavations in and around the southern kingdom have proceeded at a rapid pace, and new discoveries are coming to light with increasing frequency. The biblical records are more extensive and detailed for this period than for other periods in Israel's history. They thus shed enormous light on the archaeological material.

A central question facing archaeologists is the exact location of the walls of Jerusalem. Solomon extended the wall to the north to include the temple mount. But how far was the old Jerusalem wall extended to the west by his successors? And who extended it? Most archaeologists credit King Hezekiah with this work. In the face of the growing Assyrian threat, Hezekiah "worked hard repairing all the broken sections of the wall [of Jerusalem] and building towers on it." He also "built another wall outside that one and reinforced the supporting terraces of the City of David" (2 Chron. 32:5).

Hezekiah completed the Siloam tunnel. He first filled in all the natural wells in Judah so the invading Assyrians would not have a ready water supply. He then dug a tunnel to bring water from the spring of Gihon to a reservoir or pool inside the city wall (2 Kings 20:20; 2 Chron. 32:30). Hezekiah's tunnel still exists. An inscription commemorating its completion is located in the rock wall of the tunnel entrance. Among other things, it tells of a miscalculation of the diggers at both ends of the tunnel that nearly resulted in their tunneling past each other. The tunnel takes a circuitous route under the old City of David. The diggers followed the contours of the ground above them to minimize the distance between themselves; those on the surface signaled directions to them by pounding the ground. Fortunately, according to the inscription, when the diggers approached each other, they heard voices and began tunneling at a new angle until they met.

Hezekiah and the Assyrian Threat

After the fall of Samaria and during the early reign of Sargon II, there were many attempts at rebellion directed against Assyria. The emerging nation of Babylon gained a short-lived independence from Assyria under Merodach-Baladan (Isa. 39:1). Sargon II conducted no major military campaigns into Palestine after 720 B.C. At the same time, Egyptian power was on the rise. In the face of such a realignment of power, the various states of Syria and Palestine began asserting their own independence from Assyria. Counting on Egyptian aid (which never materialized), Ashdod, a Philistine stronghold, rebelled in 714 B.C. In 712 Sargon II's army defeated Ashdod and turned it into an Assyrian province. The fact that Judah escaped any retributive damage in this raid suggests it had taken no part in the rebellion.

During Hezekiah's sixth year (712 B.C.) the Assyrian king Shalmaneser V captured Samaria, the capital of the nothern kingdom. A few years later, during the reign of Sennacherib (704–681 B.C.), Hezekiah ceased paying tribute to Assyria (2 Kings 18:7). Sennacherib quickly responded by invading Judah and placing Jerusalem under siege.

There is a considerable amount of background information regarding Sennacherib's campaign. The Phoenician and Philistine coastal cities again openly rebelled against Assyria and sought aid from Egypt. According to Sennacherib's own account, one of the Philistine kings, Padi, king of Ekron, remained loyal to the Assyrians. A popular uprising, led by royal officials in Ekron, deposed Padi and handed him over to Hezekiah in Jerusalem for safekeeping. Sennacherib says that Hezekiah "held him in prison, unlawfully, as if he [Padi] had been an enemy" (*ANET*, p. 283). Sennacherib considered Hezekiah's act to be complicity with the Philistine cities and invaded Judah. Hezekiah apparently anticipated Sennacherib's response and thus prepared early for his invasion (see previous unit on "Archaeology of Jerusalem").

By all accounts Sennacherib's invasion resulted in mass destruction of cities in Palestine. Egypt, who initially aided the Philistine cities, was defeated near Ekron. Sennacherib then turned his armies toward Judah where, he boasts, he destroyed forty-six of Judah's fortified towns (see next unit on "Lachish"). The siege of Jerusalem came in 701 B.C. This was the primary occasion for the prophet Isaiah to make his plea to the king and the people of Judah to trust in God's deliverance (2 Kings 18–19). Hezekiah responded, and God delivered his kingdom from the grip of the Assyrian king. The Bible says only that the Assyrians were annihilated by the angel of the Lord (2 Kings 19:35; 2 Chron. 32:20–23). The ancient historian Herodotus reports they were stricken by a deadly plague. As might be expected, Sennacherib makes no mention of this defeat. The only thing he admits is that he surrounded Jerusalem and held Hezekiah barricaded "like a bird in a cage" (*ANET*, p. 287).

Lachish

A graphic portrayal of Sennacherib's destruction of the Judean city of Lachish (cf. 2 Kings 18:14) has been found on the walls of his royal palace excavated at Nineveh (*ANEP*, no. 372). A close study of this majestic stone relief reveals much about the art and cruelty of ancient warfare. Sennacherib and his army are in the heat of battle. The momentum is clearly on the Assyrian side. The defenders of Lachish are fighting for their lives against overwhelming odds.

The walls of Lachish are still intact. Its defensive bowmen, stationed atop towers placed at regular intervals in the wall, shoot down upon their attackers. Assyrian foot soldiers stand ready to scale the wall on wooden ramparts. Along the top of the wall are stationed Judean soldiers hurling firebrands and slinging stones down on the Assyrians. At the center of the picture stands a large siege machine with a battering rod extending out its front side. Behind this machine, which looks strangely like a modern tank, Assyrian bowmen shoot furiously at those on the wall.

The picture leaves no doubt about the outcome of the battle. Already captives are being led out of the city gates, and captured fugitives hang impaled on large wooden stakes. Given the graphic detail of the Assyrian artisan who recorded this scene of battle, the biblical narrative's simple statement, "Sennacherib king of Assyria attacked all the fortified cities of Judah and captured them" (2 Kings 18:13), seems the height of understatement. It is remarkable that we should have today, after over 2,500 years, an official "photograph" of a significant battle in one of the most important military campaigns recounted in the Bible. It is in examples such as this that we see not only that the Bible has given us an accurate account of Israel's history, but also that the events recorded in the Bible actually happened to real people at specific times. The biblical narratives are not mere stories; they are stories about real events and real people.

Moreover, excavations in the city of Lachish itself confirm the brutality of this battle against the Assyrians. Archaeologists have found several large pits containing the decapitated and burned remains of at least 1,500 bodies, covered with a layer of pig bones.

Real People and Places in Inscriptions

Another reminder that the Bible is about real people and real places is the discovery and subsequent decipherment of the tomb inscription of Hezekiah's "prime minister," Shebna (Isa. 22:15). The tomb is one of several carved out of the rock hillside of Silwan, just outside Jerusalem. The prophet Isaiah spoke harshly of Shebna's building himself such an opulent tomb. For his part, Shebna's inscription suggests that he too was concerned about the appearance of wealth that such an elaborate tomb would give to those who survived him. His inscription reads, "There is no silver or gold here, only bones."

Mention should be made here again to the 1993 discovery of an Aramaic inscription in the northern city of Dan dated 850 B.C. and bearing the words "the house of David" (see the unit entitled "David's Kingdom"). This text represents the first occurrence of the name "David" outside the Bible. Other inscriptions bear what are likely the names of kings from the southern kingdom of Judah. An official seal, uncovered in the southern port city of Ezion Geber, has the Hebrew words inscribed on it "belonging to Jotham." Jotham's father, Uzziah, the king of Judah, "rebuilt Elath and restored it to [the kingdom of] Judah" (2 Kings 14:22). Another Judean seal bears the name "Manasseh, son of the king." If this is Manasseh, the son of Hezekiah, it would have been used by him in early childhood since he became king at the age of twelve.

Houses in Jerusalem from the latter days of the southern kingdom have recently been excavated on the eastern ridge of the city. In one house were found several clay impressions used to seal papyrus documents and inscribed with personal names. The name of "Gemariah, the son of Shaphan," an important scribe mentioned in Jeremiah 36:10, was among these. Another name that shows up on a series of recently discovered seals is Jeremiah's own secretary, "Baruch, son of Neriah." Baruch was the scribe who recorded the book of Jeremiah from the words of the prophet (Jer. 36:4). On one of the seals, which was made from an impression in soft clay, Baruch's thumb print can still be seen. It is thus remarkable to think that we have the very thumb print of one of the biblical authors who lived over 2,500 years ago.

Finally, during the reign of Rehoboam (922–915 B.C.), Shishak, an Egyptian king, launched a massive invasion of the lands of Syria and Canaan (1 Kings 14:25–28). Shishak recorded the invasion on the walls of the temple at Karnak, listing over 150 cities and towns that he captured. Shishak unfortunately did not provide a narrative of this campaign. But a fragment of a victory stele uncovered at Megiddo confirms the general reliability of his list. Archaeological evidence suggests that most of the cities of Canaan were destroyed in the invasion, including the royal fortifications along Judah's southern border.

Religion and Education in the Southern Kingdom

Early in the kingdom of Judah the people began to neglect the law of Moses. In the eyes of the biblical writers, their apostasy was most visible in their adoption of "high places" for worship. Such places were not located in Jerusalem at the temple site, but in scattered local shrines and altars throughout the kingdom. Built of mounds of stones, the high places were commonly used in Canaanite religion and had apparently been adopted by the Israelites, much to the chagrin of the prophets. Not only did worship at such sites violate the explicit command in the Law that Israel was to worship God only at the temple, but they also frequently contained large stones, or "sacred pillars," and other representations of gods of the sort that were expressly prohibited in the Ten Commandments.

We are not told to what extent the adoption of these practices meant the complete acceptance of the ideas and practices of Canaanite religion. In times of national revival, however, these high places became a primary target. Judah's two greatest kings, Hezekiah and Josiah, established programs to eradicate the high places from the land. Because they were constructed of stone mounds, some have survived intact in the ruins of the cities of the southern and northern kingdoms.

Throughout the history of the southern kingdom, a series of fortifications and defensive outposts were built and maintained on its southern borders, from which we can gain a rather complete picture of life during this time. The city of Arad, for example, contained a "sanctuary" with a sacrificial altar that was destroyed at the time of Hezekiah's reform, while the sanctuary itself was destroyed at the time of Josiah's reforms. Such details confirm in remarkable details the historical accuracy of the biblical narratives.

Reading and writing continued throughout Judah. Numerous writing exercise tablets and inscriptions have come to light. As in other ancient cultures, writing exercises concentrated on learning the proper forms and sequence of the Hebrew alphabet. In many exercise tablets, drawings are found alongside alphabetic inscriptions; these are perhaps an early form of doodling. Some of these writing exercises have also been found on the walls and steps of buildings. Apparently students were encouraged to practice the alphabet on any available surface.

The Evidence of the Ostraca

In the coastal town of Yavneh-Yam, an ostracon from late seventh century B.C. has been uncovered that contains the plea (in the literary form of a lament psalm) of a poor farmer for justice from the governor. The farmer, after he had completed most of his work and had stored his grain, was accosted by a certain Hoshaiah son of Shobai, possibly his foreman. Hoshaiah took the farmer's cloak and would not return it. The farmer pleads with the governor for the return of his cloak, appealing to the testimony of his companions as to the truth of his words and insisting the governor hear his case. This plea provides a remarkable view into the everyday affairs of preexilic Judah. The farmer's plight is similar to that addressed by Exodus 22:26–27, according to which, when a cloak was given as collateral, it had to be returned at night to provide warmth for its owner. The farmer's plea in this ostracon puts a human face on the Mosaic law. It also sheds light on the plight of the poor and the responsibility of Israel's leaders to administer justice.

Excavations in the southern fortress of Arad (destroyed by Nebuchadnezzar's armies in 598 B.C.) have produced numerous ostraca on which are written personal letters and documents. These writings provide a revealing look into life in Judah from the early time of the divided monarchy down to the last days before the Exile. In the top layer of occupation, stored away in a room covered by a thick burnt layer (indicating the house was probably destroyed by fire), seventeen ostraca were found, all addressed to the same individual, Eliashib son of Ishyahu. They dealt with daily rations of food. In effect, these documents served as "order forms" for specific quantities of food that Eliashib apparently supplied to army troops along the southern borders of Judah. Eliashib kept these ostraca as receipts of his transactions, probably intending to record them in his files of papyrus documents (such documents would have perished long ago). Often supplies in Eliashib's records are earmarked for a group of soldiers called the "Kittim," the Hebrew word at that time for Greek mercenaries. Here, before our very eyes, stand documents representing the long-forgotten details of the everyday lives of ancient Israel.

In the Judean city of Lachish, southwest of Jerusalem, several ostraca from the last days of the Judean kingdom, written in Hebrew, tell of military preparations for the coming attack by Babylon. In one text we have a dispatch report sent from an outpost to the leaders of the city of Lachish. The report informs the city that the fire signals from a nearby city, Azekah, cannot be seen. The meaning of this report is still being debated. Perhaps Azekah has already been destroyed by the Babylonians, or else the fire signals have not yet been lit.

The Rise of Babylon

Increasingly beset by internal strife, the Assyrian empire hardly outlived its last great ruler, Asshurbanapal (d. 627 B.C.). Nineveh, its capital, fell to a coalition of Babylonians and Medes in 612 B.C. The Assyrians retreated westward to Haran near the Euphrates River with the Babylonian forces in hot pursuit. By 610 the Babylonians had ousted them from that last stronghold. The final battle came in 609, when the Babylonian army decimated the Assyrians at Carchemish, a city on the west bank of the Euphrates. The ill-timed help offered by the Egyptians proved futile. That may have been because the Egyptians, led by King Neco, had been delayed by an encounter with the Judean king Joshiah. Joshiah lost his life, but by confronting the Egyptians on their way to rescue Assyria, he may have tilted the scales slightly in favor of the Babylonians. In doing so, he also sealed the fate of his own kingdom of Judah. It was to be Babylon, not Assyria or Egypt, that brought his kingdom to its knees.

Having defeated Assyria, the Babylonians turned their forces against their last rival, Egypt. Egypt was defeated in the Battle of Carchemish (605 B.C.). According to Babylonian records, Nebuchadnezzar "marched to Carchemish which lay on the bank of the river Euphrates. He crossed the river [to go] against the Egyptian army which was situated in Carchemish. ... They fought with each other and the Egyptian army withdrew before him. ... Not a single person escaped to his own country." The Bible also gives us a clear view of this same battle: "The king of Egypt did not march out of his own country again, because the king of Babylon had taken all his territory, from the Wadi of Egypt to the Euphrates River" (2 Kings 24:7).

While still in Syria-Palestine, Nebuchadnezzar got word of his father's (Nebopolassar) death and returned to Babylon to take his throne. According to Daniel 1:1–3, Judean captives, including Daniel and his friends, were carried off to Babylon at this time. In the following year, Nebuchadnezzar returned to Syria-Palestine. It is generally assumed that the note in 2 Kings 24:1 is to be dated from this period: "Nebuchadnezzar king of Babylon invaded the land, and Jehoiakim became his vassal for three years." As the remainder of the verse suggests, however, Jehoiakim then rebelled against Nebuchadnezzar, probably at the time that Nebuchadnezzar suffered a major defeat by the Egyptians. According to the Babylonian Chronicle, "In the year [601 B.C.] the king of Akkad [Babylon] called up his army and went to Hatti [Syria-Palestine]. He went through Hatti in power. In Kislev [Nov./Dec. 601], he put himself at the head of his troops and set out for Egypt. The king of Egypt heard of this and called up his troops; they joined in a battle and inflicted a great defeat. The king of Akkad and his army turned and went back to Babylon" (*ANET*, p. 277).

After this defeat, Nebuchadnezzar prepared his army for the next two years. Then in 598 B.C. he returned to Syria-Palestine, intent on punishing

Jehoiakim. In that same year Jehoiakim died and was replaced by his son Jehoiachin. After only a three-month reign in Jerusalem, Nebuchadnezzar besieged the city (597) and took Jehoiachin captive to Babylon. He also plundered the Jerusalem temple, taking many treasures with him back to Babylon. Jehoiachin was replaced by his uncle Mattaniah, whose name was changed to Zedekiah (2 Kings 24:17). This was the second exile to Babylon.

The Fall of Jerusalem

The last days of the kingdom of Judah began with the reign of Zedekiah. The primary sources for the history of this period are the biblical historical books and the book of Jeremiah. Second Kings 24:18–20 tells us only briefly that Zedekiah "did evil in the eyes of the LORD" and that he "rebelled against the king of Babylon [Nebuchadnezzar]." During this time the prophet Jeremiah kept encouraging the survivors in Jerusalem to submit to the rule of Babylon and accept the impending exile as God's righteous judgment on the nation. Many others, however, spoke out strongly against Jeremiah's message. They counseled King Zedekiah to rebel against Babylon. Unfortunately, Zedekiah heeded their advice. After nine years as king, in 588 B.C., he rebelled against Babylon and, apparently, sought help from Egypt (Jer. 37:5–11). Nebuchadnezzar responded by besieging Jerusalem (2 Kings 25:1)—a siege that lasted until 586.

Having placed a blockade around the city of Jerusalem, Nebuchadnezzar began a systematic attack on the Judean cities around Jerusalem. Archaeological excavations give us an interesting glimpse of these last days of the Davidic monarchy. Jeremiah 34:6 records that only two Judean fortresses were left, Lachish and Azekah, but these too fell. (On the excavations at Lachish from this time period, see the unit on "The Evidence of the Ostraca.")

In the summer of 586 B.C., the Babylonian siege of Jerusalem came to its inevitable conclusion. Nebuchadnezzar's army broke through the walls of the city and entered it. Zedekiah and his elite troops fled to the nearby city of Jericho under cover of night (2 Kings 25:4), making use of a secret passageway in the city wall. The Babylonians were quick to hunt them down, however. Zedekiah was brought, bound in chains, to Nebuchadnezzar at Riblah in the north. His sons were slain before his eyes and he was then blinded. Still bound in chains, Zedekiah was taken to Babylon. We do not hear of him again.

A month after the initial breakthrough at Jerusalem, the Babylonians razed the city to the ground. More captives were taken to Babylon—those, that is, who were not slain in a wholesale slaughter at Riblah (2 Kings 25:18–21). In the aftermath of the conquest of Jerusalem, Judah was made a province of the Babylonian empire, and a governor named Gedaliah was commissioned. A seal dating from this period and bearing the name "Gedaliah" has been uncovered, identifying him as "one who is over the house." The seal may come from a period in Gedaliah's life before he became governor. The capital of the region over which he was appointed was moved to the centrally located Mizpah. Not long after that, Gedaliah himself was assassinated and the remaining Judeans, fearing for their lives, fled to Egypt. They forced Jeremiah to go with them.

The Exile
and the Postexilic Period

Life in Palestine and Egypt After 586 B.C.

Archaeological evidence from this period reveals massive destruction at every major fortified city in the southern kingdom. Those cities were not rebuilt for many years. Most of the population had died of starvation, been killed in battle, or been deported to Babylon or Egypt. There remained settled populations in Samaria, Galilee, and the Transjordan, and it is these that we read of again during the days when the exiles returned to Palestine. Little is known of the historical events in Palestine during the time of the Exile.

We know from 2 Kings 25:26 that many of the citizens of the southern kingdom, left behind by the Babylonians, fled to Egypt in the days following the destruction of Jerusalem (cf. Jer. 42–44). The prophet Jeremiah himself was also taken to Egypt—although he had warned the people that they should stay in Judah and trust in the Lord to save them from Babylon. It was apparently from this group of exiles that the Jewish military colony at Elephantine in the fifth century was formed. Several letters from that colony, written in Aramaic, were discovered in Egypt at the turn of this century. They show that a thriving community of Jewish exiles continued to exist in that region throughout much of the remaining centuries of the pre-Christian era.

Life in Babylon After 586 B.C.

The Jews taken into Babylonian captivity made up what might be called the upper strata of Judean society. Many had been well educated and had assumed important leadership roles in the preexilic community, including political and religious roles. According to 2 Kings 24:14, 10,000 captives were taken in 598 B.C. with Jehoiachin. Second Kings 25:11 does not give the number of Jews taken in the 586 B.C. exile; it states only that the Babylonians took all those remaining in Jerusalem into exile, some of whom were executed at Riblah (25:18–21). According to Jeremiah 52:28–30, the number of male exiles for all of Nebuchadnezzar's campaigns was about 4,600. There were, then, at most about 20,000 exiles in Babylon as a result of Nebuchadnezzar's campaigns.

Once in Babylon, the Jewish exiles settled in regions of their own. Ezekiel 3:15 mentions the settlement of Tel Abib, beside the River Kebar. Ezra 2:59 and 8:17 also mention sites where the exiles settled in Babylon, where they were allowed to build houses and plant gardens (Jer. 29:5–6). The Judean king, Jehoiachin, was treated with great respect during his captivity in Babylon—at least during the reign of Evil-Merodach (2 Kings 25:27–30; Jer. 52:31–34), though during the time of Nebuchadnezzar, he was held in prison. There are a few references to the activities of the exiles scattered through the prophecies of Jeremiah (ch. 29) and Ezekiel (8:1; 14:1; 33:30–31). Apart from such brief notes, the only full account of the activities of the exiles is the book of Daniel (Esther is to be dated after the Exile).

The Last Days of the Babylonian Empire

After the destruction of Jerusalem in 586 B.C., Nebuchadnezzar continued to carry on military campaigns into Palestine. In 585 he besieged Tyre and blockaded the city for thirteen years (cf. Ezek. 26:7). He was forced to abandon his siege because Tyre had taken up a secure position on its island fortress (cf. Ezek. 29:17–20). In 582, Nebuchadnezzar again entered Palestine and, according to Jeremiah 52:30, carried off more exiles to Babylon. In 568 he invaded Egypt. After his death in 562, the Babylonian empire rapidly declined in power.

The last king of Babylon was Nabonidus (555–539 B.C.). He transferred his residence from Babylon to the Arabian desert oasis of Teima. He remained there ten years, leaving his son, Belshazzar, in charge at Babylon (*ANET*, pp. 313–14; cf. Dan. 5). In doing this, Nabonidus failed to appear during the annual New Year's Day rite in Babylon. This greatly angered the religious leaders in Babylon and ultimately led to their disloyalty to him in favor of the Persian king Cyrus, who together with the Medes took over the empire.

The Medes and Persians are first mentioned in the written records of the Assyrian king Shalmaneser III (836 B.C.). They were part of a large migration of Indo-Ayrian peoples from the northeast into the plateau region of Iran. Shalmaneser received tribute from kings of a people known as the *Parsua[scaron]*. Those Indo-Ayrian groups split into two larger groups, the Medes and the Persians. The Medes remained in the northern plateau area where they had originally settled, while the Persians moved south.

These Iranian people first became a unified force in the ancient world under the Median king Cyaxares II (625–585 B.C.). Cyaxares made a military alliance with Nabopolasser of Babylon, and together they crushed the Assyrians, destroying Nineveh in 612 and Haran in 610–609. Cyaxares soon extended his boundaries into Asia Minor, attacking and ultimately defeating the Lydians. After a prolonged war, the Median kingdom established its western boundaries at the River Halys in Asia Minor. Cyaxares was succeeded by Astyages (585–550), who gave his daughter, Mandane, to the Persian king Cambyses. From that marriage came a son, Kura[scaron]—known today as Cyrus the Great.

Cyrus the Great

Cyrus (550–530 B.C.) united the Persian tribes and conquered the Medes. In doing so he established the first stage of the Persian empire. He set out to further his empire in Asia Minor. In 547, he defeated Sardis and annexed the rest of Asia Minor to his empire.

At this same time, Cyrus was also extending the borders of his empire east as far as parts of India. By the time Nabonidus had become king of Babylon, Cyrus had built Persia into a huge empire, extending from Asia Minor to India. Sensing the time was right, he turned his armies against Babylon. He first met with the Babylonian army at Ophis on the Tigris River, north of the city of Babylon. There Cyrus's general, Gobryas, crushed the Babylonian forces. There was little now to keep Cyrus out of Babylon. In 539 B.C., the Persian army entered Babylon without resistance. With the fall of Babylon, Cyrus became emperor of the largest empire in history.

It was the policy of the Persians under Cyrus to promote a kind of religious toleration (*ANET*, pp. 314–16). He issued his Edict of Restoration in the first year of his reign (Ezra 1:1), which included the rebuilding of the temple in Jerusalem. Cyrus said, "The LORD, the God of heaven, has given me all the kingdoms of the earth and he has appointed me to build a temple for him in Jerusalem in Judah" (Ezra 1:2).

Such a statement raises the question to what extent Cyrus himself actually believed that Yahweh, the God of Israel, had given him all the kingdoms of the world. On the basis of the prophecies of Isaiah, 200 years earlier, these words of Cyrus have a ring of truth about them—Yahweh, the Creator of heaven and earth, had given all the world into Cyrus's hand (Isa. 45:1–7) and appointed him to build his temple in Jerusalem (44:28). Isaiah 45:4–5, however, tells us something about Cyrus's own attitude toward Yahweh, that although this pagan king had been specifically chosen and anointed by Yahweh to carry out his plan for Judah and Jerusalem, he himself did not *know* Yahweh as the true and only God: "I summon you by name and bestow on you a title of honor; though you do not acknowledge me."

It is interesting to note that in one of his inscriptions, Cyrus states that the Babylonian god Marduk looked throughout all the countries, searching for a righteous man willing to take the place of the Babylonian king Nabonidus, because Nabonidus had forsaken the worship of Marduk for the moon god Sin. Marduk thus gave him rulership over all the world ("Then he pronounced the name of Cyrus, king of Anshan, and declared him to become the ruler of all the world"). Cyrus goes on to state that Marduk commissioned him to reestablish all the temples of the gods of Mesopotamia that the Babylonian king Nabonidus destroyed (*ANET*, pp. 315–16).

Persian Rulers Following Cyrus

Cambyses (530–522 B.C.) was the son of Cyrus. He came to the throne August 31, 530 after a brief coregency. Cambyses extended the Persian empire into Egypt in 525. Returning from Egypt, he heard that a rebellion had occurred in Persia. He died in Syria before he could return to suppress the rebellion.

Darius (521–486 B.C.), one of Cambyses' bodyguards, returned to Persia and successfully put down the rebellion. He marched through Palestine in 519 on his way to Egypt. In Egypt he assumed full control as an official monarch and completed a "Suez Canal" that connected the Mediterranean Sea with the Indian Ocean. During his reign the Greeks began to assume a role in international affairs. Darius spent much time and effort securing his borders alongside the Greek city-states. In 490 Darius fought the Greeks from Athens at Marathon and was defeated.

Xerxes (or Ahasuerus, 486–465 B.C.) was the son of Darius. The greatest challenge facing him when he came to the throne was what to do with the rising power of the Greeks. In 480 Xerxes set out with a great naval fleet and his army. He was at first successful in gaining control of Athens and the Attica Peninsula. But he made the serious mistake of burning the city of Athens. That barbaric act served to unite not only the Athenians, but also the other Greek states. On September 22, 480 B.C., Xerxes let his fleet attack the Greeks on the Isthmus of Corinth, through the narrow strait of Salamis. It was a tragic mistake. Xerxes' fleet was defeated. According to Herodotus, Xerxes lost half his fleet. He then retreated to his homeland, and little is known of the events of his reign after that time. According to Herodotus, Xerxes spent his later years living among his harem. During this part of his reign, the events of the book of Esther occurred. Ultimately, Xerxes fell victim to an assassin.

Artaxerxes (465–424 B.C.) was the son of Xerxes, assuming the throne after his father's murder. He was the king who allowed Ezra to return to Jerusalem and his cupbearer, Nehemiah, to visit Jerusalem and repair its walls. During his reign, Egypt revolted from Persian rule; hence Artaxerxes had a special interest in the affairs of Palestine.

Babylon:
Nebuchadnezzar (562 B.C.)
Amel-marduk (562–560 B.C.) = Evil-Merodach (2 Kings 25:27–30)
Nergal-shar-usur (Neriglissar) (560–556 B.C.)
Labashi-marduk (556/55 B.C.)
Nabonidus (Nabu-na'id) (555–539 B.C.)

Persia:
Cyrus (550–530 B.C.)
Cambyses (530–522 B.C.)
Darius (521–486 B.C.)
Xerxes (486–465 B.C.)
Artaxerxes I (Longimanus) (465–424 B.C.)
Ezra (458 B.C.) 7th year
Nehemiah (445 B.C.) 20th year
Ezra (428 B.C.) 37th year
Artaxerxes II (404–358 B.C.)

The Return From Exile I

During the time of the Return, Judah belonged to the Persian empire. The empire was divided into twenty districts called satrapies, each of which was governed by a satrap and divided into smaller provinces, ruled by a governor. Palestine belonged to the satrapy called "Beyond the River"—a general geographical term that included Syria, Phoenicia, and Palestine. The satrap of this region during the reign of Darius was Tattenai (cf. Ezra 5:3).

The newly appointed governor of Judah was Sheshbazzar (cf. Ezra 5:14). His local title was "Prince of Judah" (cf. 1:8). Sheshbazzar was replaced by Zerubbabel as governor of Judah (cf. Hag. 1:1; Ezra 3:2; Neh. 12:1). Zerubbabel was the son of Shealtiel and thus the grandson of King Jehoiachin (1 Chron. 3:17). Thus Judah was granted the status of a province and was allowed a governor who was a descendant of the royal family of David. Other governors during the Persian period were Nehemiah (Neh. 5:14, ca. 445–425 B.C.) and, according to the Elephantine papyri, Bagohi. The Bible also mentions provinces bordering Judah (Neh. 2:19): Samaria, governed by Sanballat during the time of Nehemiah; Ammon, governed by Tobiah; Arabia, governed by Geshem; and Ashdod.

In 538 B.C. Cyrus issued a decree to rebuild the temple in Jerusalem (Ezra 1:1–4; cf. 6:2–5). In response to that decree, a group of Jews left Babylon for Palestine. This group consisted of the "family heads of Judah and Benjamin" and the priests and Levites who had been stirred up by God to go (1:5). They were supported by a freewill offering from those Jews who remained behind. Sheshbazzar, their leader (1:11), had been entrusted with the articles of the temple that Cyrus was returning to Jerusalem (1:8).

A group of 29,166 persons came from Babylon with Zerubbabel (Ezra 2). Some of the returnees were unable to give evidence of their family's genuine Israelite descent in spite of their search for the ancestral registration (2:62). The priests among this group were prohibited from eating of the most holy things until a decision was reached regarding their lineage (2:63).

In the seventh month of that same year (538 B.C.), all the returned exiles gathered in Jerusalem, and Jeshua the priest and Zerubbabel built an altar to offer burnt offerings (Ezra 3:1–3). They celebrated the Feast of Booths according to the law of Moses (3:4). The foundation of the temple had not yet been laid (3:6), but they ordered the building materials (3:7).

In the second year of their return (536 B.C.), Zerubbabel and Jeshua and the rest of their brothers began the work of rebuilding the temple (Ezra 3:8), starting with the foundation (3:11). When their enemies, the "people of the land," heard of the rebuilding of the temple, they wanted to help, but Zerubbabel and Jeshua refused their offer (4:3). They then tried to discourage the rebuilding of the temple and were, in fact, successful until the time of the reign of Darius, sixteen years later (cf. 4:4–5; 6:15), when the prophets Haggai and Zechariah began to stir up the people to continue the work (5:1–2). The satrap of "Beyond the River" tried to halt the building of the temple by sending a letter to the Persian king, Darius, requesting confirmation of the permit given the Jews to rebuild the temple. This was, in effect, a request for a copy of the Edict of Restoration issued by Cyrus. Darius had the records searched in the capital city of Ecbatana, and a copy of the edict was recovered (6:1–5). Darius thus commanded that the Jews be allowed to complete their work on the temple (Ezra 6:7–12). In 516 B.C. the temple was completed (6:15).

Esther, Ezra, and Nehemiah

The events of the book of Esther fall between the building of the temple and the activities of Ezra—between Ezra 6 and 7 (a period of 58 years), the time of the Persian king Xerxes (Ahasuerus, 486–465 B.C.). It was a difficult time for the Persian empire, for in 480, the Greeks defeated the Persians at Salamis, and a year later they suffered further losses at Plateau. After that battle, Xerxes remained in Susa, his capital, where we find him in the book of Esther.

Esther (Hadassah) and Mordecai were descendants of Jews who were taken to Babylon with Jehoiachin (597 B.C.). In the seventh year of Xerxes (479), Esther was taken into Xerxes' royal palace and became queen (Est. 2:16–17). This was the year that Xerxes returned from his defeats by the Greeks. Presumably the Jews living in Palestine felt the impact of the decree of Xerxes ordering the death of all Jews and the seizing of their property (3:13).

The Persian king Artaxerxes granted Ezra a special request to lead a group of Jews back to Jerusalem in his seventh year (458 B.C.; Ezra 7:6–7). Ezra was a scribe, skilled in the law of Moses (7:6). He was a Levite and a descendant of Aaron (7:5). His mission in going to Jerusalem seems to have been to establish law and order in Judah as prescribed by the Torah (7:25–26). Thus he was to appoint magistrates and judges to enforce and teach the Torah (7:25–26). Ezra was accompanied by 1,754 men (ch. 8).

The events recorded in the book of Nehemiah occurred thirteen years later, in the twentieth year of Artaxerxes (445 B.C.; Neh. 1:1). Nehemiah was a cupbearer to Artaxerxes at his palace in Susa (1:11). He heard a report that conditions were still grave for the returnees. The remnant was in great distress, the wall of Jerusalem was "broken down," and the gates were burned (1:3; cf. 2 Kings 25). That same year Nehemiah was appointed governor of the province of Judah (Neh. 5:14) and was commissioned by Artaxerxes to repair the walls of Jerusalem (2:8). He arrived in Jerusalem with a written order from Artaxerxes and was accompanied by the king's army and cavalry (2:9). He met with immediate opposition from other governors of "Beyond the River" (2:10, 19–20)—Sanballat of Samaria and Tobiah of Ammon. In spite of the opposition, Nehemiah armed his workers, and they completed the walls without further incident (4:13–23).

The Intertestamental Period (445–168 B.C.)

The time from Ezra and Nehemiah (445 B.C.) to the Maccabean Revolt (168 B.C.) is one of the least documented periods of the Old Testament era. Under the administration of the Persian empire, Palestine was an important staging and supply area for the Persian armies, particularly those keeping a watchful eye on Egypt. Agriculture had become a chief concern as the population moved away from the large cities and into the countryside. Many of the cities occupied in the preexilic period were abandoned during this time. Some became ideal for centrally located storage bins.

Typical archaeological methods, such as excavation of ancient mounds of cities (tells), have consequently proved inadequate as the sole, or even most important, source of our knowledge of this period. Recent surface surveys over wide geographical areas have, however, begun to show a more definite profile of the population and culture of this period. This new data, mixed with evidence from those cities that were occupied during this period, suggests that Palestine was divided along two distinct cultural influences. In the central and southern hill country and in the eastern, Transjordan area, cultural life appears to have preserved much of its preexilic character. There is little to distinguish the material culture of this region from its earlier occupants prior to the Exile. Those who settled in these remote areas continued the old ways developed under the influence of Assyrian, Babylonian, and Egyptian domination.

In the north, however—that is, in Galilee—and along the coastline, the beginning stages of Greek culture were well on their way to transforming life in Palestine. Hellenization, (i.e., the spread of Greek ideas and culture into the world of the ancient Near East) had already begun in this region under the rule of the Persians. There was thus already a cultural base on which the spread of Greek culture under Alexander the Great could build. In the eastern, Transjordan area, life continued much as it had before the fall of Jerusalem.

The Persians appear to have governed Palestine largely through local officials. At key points throughout the land official outposts were maintained, usually at strategically important sites within existing cities and towns. Such sites were maintained in the north at Hazor, in the center at Jerusalem, and in the south at Lachish.

There is considerable evidence of writing in Palestine during the Persian period. Silver coins issued by local authorities in Jerusalem have been uncovered from the fourth century B.C., inscribed in an early Hebrew script. One such coin shows a human figure sitting on a winged chariot. In his left hand rests a hawk. Alongside such locally minted coins are many official Persian coins. Official documents of the Persian empire were written in Aramaic on ostraca and papyrus. Though few papyrus texts have survived, many clay seals that once encased those documents have been found. They reveal a rich and well organized administrative system.

Outside Palestine, a collection of Aramaic documents from Egypt sheds much light on life both inside and outside the land. These documents are primarily letters written by a Jewish military colony at Elephantine on the Nile River. The members of the colony were apparently Jewish mercenary soldiers serving under the Persian government. They also appear to have been well established in Egypt before the time of the Exile. The letters show that they carried on close communication with Jewish authorities in Palestine. Many details of life in Palestine can be drawn from the letters.

The Rise of the Greeks

The last Persian king was Darius III (335–330 B.C.). When he came to the throne, he was faced with two major problems. His administrative government, centered in the organization of satrapies, was in disarray, and the Greeks, led by Alexander the Great, were pushing hard on his borders. Darius was successful in dealing with the first problem, but not the second. In 334 Alexander's army crossed over into Asia Minor and defeated the Persians at the River Granicus in northwest Asia Minor. In 333, Alexander defeated the Persians a second time at Issus, the gateway into the Near East.

Alexander then moved his troops southward into Syria-Palestine on his way to Egypt. He besieged the Phoenician city of Tyre for seven months, constructing a stone bridge from the mainland to the fortress island, and eventually defeated the Phoenicians. Alexander entered Egypt unopposed in 332. During that campaign, the district of Judah submitted without resistance. Alexander went on from there to conquer the whole of the Persian empire, defeating Darius for the last time in 331 and passing on to the Indus Valley (327). Four years later, in 323, Alexander became ill and died in Babylon.

With the death of Alexander, the newly formed Greek empire collapsed. Most of it was divided between two of his generals—Ptolemy, who took Egypt, and Seleucus, who took Babylon, Mesopotamia, and Syria. Ptolemy's capital was in Alexandria in Egypt, and Seleucus' two capitals were in Seleucia, on the Tigris River, and Antioch, in northern Syria. Palestine was ruled by the Ptolemies for the next one hundred years. In 198 B.C, the Seleucid empire, under Antiochus IV (223–187), defeated the Ptolemies and gained control of Palestine.

Hellenization

With the expansion of the Greek empire under Alexander came a systematic attempt to unite all the known world, East and West, into a single, well-defined culture. Alexander arranged mass marriages between his Greek troops and local native populations. He also began a process of establishing Greek-speaking settlements throughout his conquered territories. Each colony became an active center for the spread of the Greek language and culture.

During the course of the fourth and third centuries B.C., the Jews who lived in Palestine were confronted with strong pressures to rethink their traditional beliefs in terms of "modern" Greek cultural ideas. That process was known as Hellenization. One of the most important steps in that process was the exportation from Palestine of thousands of Jews to Egypt (ca. 300 B.C.). These Jews were responsible for translating the Hebrew Scriptures into Greek. That translation, called the Septuagint, not only introduced Greek culture into the interpretation of the Bible, but also introduced the Bible and its ideas to the non-Hebrew-speaking world.

Such mergers of the world of the Bible with the Greek world were often met with stiff opposition, especially from relugous leaders who wished to remain faithful to the earlier Hebrew traditions. In the first stages of this conflict of cultures lie the roots of the two groups known as the Pharisees and Sadducees. The Pharisees stressed the need for Hellenization. The Sadducees, though certainly affected by Hellenism, ultimately remained more true to the ancient Hebrew traditions. The most significant confrontation of Hellenism and ancient tradition came in the form of the Maccabean Revolt (168 B.C.). This was, in fact, a confrontation between traditional Judaism and Greek pagan religion. The religious Jews united against the syncretism and paganism that was forced on them by their Greek overlords. This struggle continued into the New Testament era.

The Life of Christ

Caesar, Quirinius, and the Census

According to Luke, Jesus was born during the time when Caesar ordered a census, in which everyone was required to return to their ancestral home to be registered. To further date it, Luke adds that this was the first census "when Quirinius was governor of Syria" (Luke 2:1–3). Years ago scholars faulted Luke on several accounts: that we have no record such a census ever took place, that people never had to travel to their ancestral home for registration, and that Quirinius became governor of Syria ten years after the supposed birth of Christ.

First, it is important to recognize that Jesus was born somewhere between 6 and 4 B.C. In the sixth century, Dionysius Exiguus (a monk skilled in mathematics and astronomy) took it upon himself to reform the calendar by dating everything from the birth of Christ. However, despite careful work, he erred in his calculations. He determined that Jesus was born 753 years after the founding of Rome, but later calculations now make it clear that Herod the Great died 749 years after that date. Jesus was clearly born before the death of Herod (Matt. 2).

Papyrus documents discovered early in the twentieth century indicate that the Romans took a census every fourteen years. Judging by the dates of known censuses, we can deteremine that one must have begun in about 8 B.C. Presumably the implementation of this decision did not get to the outlying areas of the Roman empire until a couple years later. Thus 6 B.C. in Palestine falls well within the possible time framework of this census.

Scholars for a long time claimed that there is no evidence that Rome required subjects to return to their ancestral homes for a census. But nearly a century ago archaeologists found an edict from an Egyptian governor who, in A.D. 104, required taxpayers to return to their original homes for registration.

It is true that Quirinius took on the governorship of Syria in A.D. 6. But in 1828 archaeologists found an inscription at Rome indicating that Quirinius was governor twice; a inscription uncovered later by William Ramsay suggests the same thing. In any case, Quirinius was a military commander in Syria much earlier than A.D. 6, and there is no reason to question that he was given a special commission to supervise the census referred to in Luke 2.

Herod the Great

When Herod the Great first began his reign, he was an exceptionally capable ruler. He had the ability to stand between Rome and the Jews (who hated subservience to Rome) and make decisions that pleased both. He beautified the land of Palestine with numerous building projects, such as fortresses, palaces, and aqueducts. One of his main achievements was the rebuilding of the temple in Jerusalem. According to Josephus, in order to make sure that the temple would not be defiled by common hands, he commissioned a thousand priests to do the construction. The main part of the temple was built from 20–19 B.C., but the final touches were still being put on forty-five years later. That is why the Jews could say, in John 2:20, "It has taken forty-six years to build this temple."

There is no independent historical or archaeological confirmation of the slaughter of the babies in Bethlehem at the time of Jesus' birth (see Matt. 2), but it certainly fits in with what we know about the latter years of Herod. Toward the end of his life, he became extremely paranoid and fearful that someone would replace him as king. On the slightest suspicion that they were plotting against him, he did not hesitate to kill his favorite wife as well as her grandfather and her mother, his brother-in-law, and three of his sons. According to Josephus, he was so worried that no one would grieve his death that he ordered that when he died, leaders from all over Judea were to be locked in the hippodrome at Jericho and then slaughtered, so there would be universal mourning.

With such a personality, the slaughter of up to twenty-five babies in Bethlehem would seem inconsequential. It is certainly entirely feasible that when Herod heard from the Magi that a "king of the Jews" had been born, he would pull out all the stops to make sure this person would never live to be old enough to assume a throne (Matt. 2:16–18). The death of Herod a few months later fits well with the biblical data concerning the flight of Joseph, Mary, and Jesus into Egypt and their subsequent return to Palestine (2:13–15, 19–20).

The Papyri

Scholars have always been aware that the Greek of the New Testament does not look like the classical Greek of Plato and Aristotle or the Greek of Jewish writers such as Josephus and Philo (contemporaries of Jesus). In general, it does not have the subtleties of grammar or the stylistic finesse of classical or literary Hellenistic Greek. Until nearly the end of the nineteenth century, some scholars called the Greek of the New Testament "Holy Ghost Greek"—a special language that the Holy Spirit devised in which to communicate God's word to humankind. One scholar found as many as 550 words that he considered to be unique "biblical words," seeing that they were unknown in any other earlier ancient sources.

But in the late nineteenth century, scholars found thousands of papyri documents from the centuries both before and after Christ—wills, letters, receipts, orders for goods, contracts, etc., most of them written in Greek and well preserved in the dry climate of Egypt. These were written in the common language spoken by the people (the Greek word for common is *koine*). Thus, in addition to Classical Greek and Hellenistic Greek, we now know a Koine Greek.

When the great scholar Adolf Deissmann compared the Greek of these papyri with the New Testament, he found grammatical structures, stylistic features, and words that were similar, if not identical. Thus, for example, dozens of words that were once thought to be unique to the New Testament are now known to be common words spoken in the Greco-Roman world.

The discover of the papyri has aided greatly in determining the meanings of the New Testament as well as in understanding the cultural world in which Jesus and the apostles lived. Take the follow word example: In 1 Peter 2:2, Peter talks about *adolon gala*, which the KJV translates as "sincere milk." In the papyri, however, *adolos* is sometimes linked with grain or oil to indicate its purity (unadulterated with impure substances). Thus, Peter is talking about "pure . . . milk" (NIV). Or take the style of letters: It is now beyond doubt that the way in which the New Testament writers composed their letters followed the conventions of letter-writing in antiquity. Each writer did, of course, give his own slant, but they were writing in a familiar style.

Jesus' Ministry

According to the Gospels, Jesus ministered mainly in Judea and Galilee, with occasional trips into Transjordan, Samaria, and other places outside Palestine. Almost all the sites that he visited have been identified today, and some of them have been excavated. These have added vastly to the knowledge we have about Jesus' world and Jesus' words.

One of Jesus' first sermons was in his hometown of Nazareth. For a long time scholars debated whether Nazareth ever had a synagogue, suggesting that what Luke wrote was a made-up story. But excavations in this city have unearthed at least three synagogues, making it entirely likely that Jesus did speak at a synagogue in that town.

One of the most famous synagogues archaeologists have uncovered is the one in Capernaum (cf. Mark 2:1; John 6:59). The remains of the top layer date from the third or fourth century A.D., but underneath are traces of a previous synagogue, which dates from the first century—perhaps the very one in which Jesus taught and performed miracles.

Close to this synagogue is the remains of an octagon building, which is almost certainly a fifth-century church; underneath it is the remains of an even earlier church. According to excavators, the central hall of this church had at one time been a house, probably from the first century B.C. But about the middle of the first century A.D., the walls of this house were plastered—the only plastered house found in Capernaum, which suggests that it had been converted into a public meeting place. On these walls are graffiti that mention Jesus as "Christ" and "Lord" (in Greek), as well as boats, crosses, and other symbols. This is probably the earliest evidence we have for a Christian worship center. Beneath the crushed limestone floor fishhooks were found.

All of this suggests that this site had long been considered important to Christians. Scholars are suggesting that this indeed may be the house of the apostle Peter (cf. Mark 1:29–31, where Jesus enters Peter's house immediately after leaving the synagogue, in order to heal Peter's mother-in-law). Peter, as we know, had been a fisherman before he accepted the call to follow Jesus. In 1987 a rather large boat that could hold as many as fifteen people, dating from Roman times, was found at the bottom of the Sea of Galilee.

Caiaphas and Pilate

One of the most exciting things a biblical archaeologist can find is an artifact that clearly and directly refers to a character in the Bible. The Gospels indicate that Jesus' trial was conducted by Caiaphas, who was high priest at that time. According to Josephus, his name was Joseph Caiaphas. In November, 1990, workers doing construction work on a slope south of the old city of Jerusalem unearthed a cave that contained twelve ossuaries (burial chests filled with bones). As archaeologists examined them, they knew immediately that these were chests from the first century A.D. In analyzing the inscriptions on the most ornate of them, they discovered the name, written in Aramaic, "Joseph son of Caiaphas." Inside the chest were, among other things, the bones of a sixty-year-old man—most likely those of the man who conducted Jesus' trial. This is the first time the bones of an actual biblical character have been identified.

The Roman governor of Palestine at the time of Jesus' trial and crucifixion was Pontius Pilate, mentioned not only in the Bible but also in Josephus and Philo. In 1961, some Italian archaeologists were excavating an ancient theater in Caesarea when they unearthed a large stone slab that had an inscription on it that read: "Pontius Pilate, Prefect of Judea, has presented the Tiberieum to the Caesareans." Apparently Pilate donated funds to Caesarea for the construction of some building.

One of the interesting things about this inscription is that Pilate is called a "prefect." Most historians, based on Josephus and others, have called him a "procuator." But we know now that Roman governors of Judea were not called procuators until later, during the reign of Claudius (A.D. 41–54). This inscription confirms that Pilate was indeed an prefect, and the New Testament accurately labels him as "governor" (*hegemon*), not a procurator.

The Crucifixion

Death by crucifixion is well attested in ancient historical sources. The Romans were not the first ones to use this slow, brutal method to kill someone. In spite of this, some scholars for a long time questioned whether any person was ever nailed to a T-shaped structure placed in the ground. They insisted that the spikes would never have held the weight of a human being but would have torn through the flesh.

But in the summer of 1968, an archaeologist was examining some Jewish ossuaries from the first century A.D. One of them, with the name Yehohanan Ben-Hagakol on it, contains the bones of a man who had obviously been crucified in the Jerusalem area. Apparently the huge spike that went through both his heels had hit a knot and curved up, so that it was impossible to removed the spike after the person died. The spike was therefore still in the foot. At the head of the spike was a sort of wooden washer, to keep the flesh from tearing out. The wrist bones in that ossuary also showed evidence of having been hit by spikes. Finally, Yehohanan's legs had been broken, probably to speed his death (cf. John 19:32).

Scholars are not agreed on precisely where Golgotha was located. The most likely place is close to where the Church of the Holy Sepulcher now stands. Even though this place stands today within the walls of the old city of Jerusalem, archaeologists have found proof that this site at one time stood immediately outside the walls of the city (cf. Heb. 13:12). And only about fifty yards away is the traditional site of the garden tomb (cf. John 19:41–42).

The Empty Tomb

Some believe it is impossible to prove beyond a shadow of a doubt that the tomb in which Jesus' body was placed after his crucifixion was empty two days later. And it is doubtless impossible to prove scientifically that, even if we could prove the tomb was empty, it was because Jesus had been raised from the dead. Our faith in the resurrected Christ does not rest on scientific evidence, nor should it. But there does seem to be some historical and archaeological evidence that helps confirm the empty tomb.

First, in Josephus, there is a segment in his *Antiquities* (18.63–64), often called the *Testimonium Flavianum*, that speaks about Jesus. Most students of Josephus acknowledge that Christian copyists embellished the actual words of Josephus, making him say, "Jesus was the Messiah . . . for he appeared alive again on the third day." But in 1972 an Arabic copy of Josephus was found, in which the disputed passage reads as follows: "His disciples . . . reported that he had appeared to them three days after his crucifixion and that he was alive; accordingly, he was perhaps the Messiah. . . ." Josephus never tries to explain away what "really" happened to the body of Jesus (as did later rabbinic sources). To have a Jew who never confessed faith in Christ write a statement of this nature suggests the authenticity of the empty tomb story.

An inscription perhaps related to Pilate's experience with Jesus was found in the city of Nazareth; it contained an order regarding grave robbery, probably written by the Roman emperor Tiberius (who ruled A.D. 14–37, when Jesus was crucified) or by Claudius (A.D. 41–54). This marble slab has a command written on it—far more detailed than any imperial edicts found to date—that graves should "remain perpetually undisturbed"; the emperor ordered an investigation and trial of anyone charged with extracting those who are buried, with transferring the body to another place, and/or with displacing the sealing of other stones of graves. The penalty for being found guilty was capital punishment (in other such edicts that have been found, the penalty was only a fine). It is significant that this edict appears in Palestine around the time of the spread of the gospel.

Perhaps the strongest historical argument for the empty tomb is the phenomenon of the early church itself. Most historians agree that something quite extraordinary must have occurred early in the history of the church to account for the overwhelming conviction of early Christians that Jesus did, in fact, arise from the grave. The empty tomb would provide just such an explanation. Secular historians, who rule out the possibility of such a miraculous event as the resurrection, have so far been unable to account to the phenomenal rise of the early church.

The Early Christian Church

Names and Places

As Christianity began to spread to other parts of the Roman empire, the book of Acts cites many different names and places. For most of these names and places there is confirmation in ancient sources of one form or another.

For example, the name of the famous Pharisee Gamaliel (Acts 5:34) is well attested in rabbinic sources as one of the greatest rabbis who lived during the same time as the New Testament. He was the grandson of Hillel, the founding father of one of the two schools of the Pharisees. Gamaliel's "liberal" view expressed in the Sanhedrin gathering fits well within what we know about the School of Hillel.

Until early in this century, the name Sapphira had not been known in any other source than Acts 5:1. In 1933, however, a report was published on an ossuary contemporary with New Testament times that had this name inscribed on it.

Though no remains of the Synagogue of the Freedmen (Freed Slaves) (Acts 6:9) have been discovered, in 1913 an inscription was found in Jerusalem, stating a certain Theodotus had constructed a synagogue. This man's father was named Vettenos (a Latin name), which suggests that at one time he had been attached, probably as a slave, to a Roman family (perhaps the family Vettius). Attached to this synagogue was a center where the needy from abroad could stay—perhaps other freed Jewish slaves who decided to move to Jerusalem.

When Philip evangelized the Ethiopian eunuch, Luke states that the eunuch was in charge of the treasury of Candace queen of the Ethiopians (Acts 8:27). Archaeological excavations in Nubia in the early twentieth century certify that there were a group of queens called "Candace"; the word (similar to "Pharaoh") was a title for the queen of the vast area south of Egypt.

What about the "Italian Regiment" that Cornelius commanded in Caesarea (Acts 10:1)? An inscription found in Caesarea, dated A.D. 69, certifies that the "Second Italian Cohort of Roman Citizen Volunteers" was stationed at Caesarea—and probably also earlier.

When Saul, after his blinding vision, entered Damascus, he went to the house of Judas on Straight Street. This street is still identifiable in Damascus (still called, in Arabic, "The Straight Way"); it is the main east-west artery through the city.

Paul's First Missionary Journey

When Paul and Barnabas set out on their first missionary journey, they began their ministry on the island of Cyprus. After traversing the island, they arrived in the capital, Paphos, where they had an opportunity to meet the proconsul, Sergius Paulus. An inscription found at Rome indicates what this man had done prior to his service on Cyprus: He was the river and flood control commissioner of the Tiber River in Italy.

Also at Cyprus was a Jewish magician-sorcerer named Elymas. Official Jewish texts, such as the Old Testament and rabbinic sources, contain strong words that are spoken against using sorcery, witchcraft, magic, necromancy, etc. But archaeologists have found many papyri and other artifacts (such as amulets) that indicate the Jews were well known and even sought after for their involvement and success in dealing with the occult (cf. also Acts 19:13–16).

Greek mythology as recorded by the Roman poet Ovid gives a clear indication of why Paul and Barnabas were venerated as gods in the city of Lystra (Acts 14:8–18). According to local legend, the two gods Zeus and Hermes had at one time visited the area in the guise of human beings. They sought lodging, but no one would take them in until an elderly couple (Philemon and Baucis) did. In appreciation, the gods turned their humble cottage into a temple with a golden roof and marble columns. The houses of those who had refused to accommodate them were destroyed. Thus, the people of Lystra, steeped in this legend, did not want to take a chance at offending the gods a second time. What could be more proof that Paul and Barnabas were gods but the healing of a man who had been crippled from birth and had never walked? Archaeologists have also found inscriptions that testify to monuments or statues both to Zeus and to Hermes in this region.

Perhaps the story at Lystra also gives a hint as to what Paul looked like. Since he was considered to be Hermes while Barnabas was Zeus, Barnabas must have been the more imposing figure and Paul much smaller and inferior in physique (cf. 2 Cor. 10:10). A presbyter of the second century described Paul as "a man small of stature, with a bald head and crooked legs . . . with eyebrows meeting and nose somewhat hooked." Early paintings in the catacombs confirm this in a general way; they present Paul as a smallish figure with a pointed, gray beard.

Paul's Second Missionary Journey

One of the most painful experiences of Paul and Silas was the beating they received in Philippi after casting the demon out of the soothsaying girl. They were then imprisoned in the city jail. One of the unique features of ancient Philippi is that no modern city occurs on the site. Thus archaeologists have been able to get a good picture of its outlay in ancient times. One of the buildings excavated is the city jail—a small stone building that almost certainly housed Paul and Silas during the night (Acts 16:22–24).

When Paul was in Athens, he went around the city on a sightseeing trip, observing the objects of the Athenians' worship (Acts 17:23). He undoubtedly toured the Acropolis, which still stands today (in ruins). It must have been an impressive tour, even though it distressed Paul greatly (Acts 17:16). Just west of the Acropolis was Mars' Hill (the Areopagus), where Paul may have delivered his message (the other possibility is that he spoke to the Council of the Areopagus). From the top of that hill one receives a masterful panoramic view of Athens.

Ancient Corinth is another place where no modern city exists. Thus excavations have been unhindered. A white marble stone was found along the Lechaion road near the central marketplace (*agora*) with the inscription, "Synagogue of the Hebrews." It is safe to assume that next door to this synagogue was the house of Titius Justus (Acts 18:7). Excavations along the southern edge of the *agora* have uncovered the large, marble-faced *bema* ("raised podium") on which Paul stood to address Gallio when the Jews hauled the apostle before the proconsul to accuse him of teaching an illegal religion.

Finally in Corinth, according to Romans 16:23, Erastus, the director of public works in Corinth (from where Paul wrote this book), sent greetings to believers in Rome. In the plaza near the ruins of the amphitheater in Corinth a limestone slab was found with this inscription: "Erastus in his aedileship laid this pavement at his own expense." This is probably the same man.

Political Terminology in Acts

One of the remarkable features of Luke's writing in Acts is the accuracy with which he uses political terminology. Luke, for example, talks about Philippi as being in the "district [*meris*] of Macedonia." The famous biblical scholar F. J. A. Hort insisted, based on knowledge of Greek at the time, that the word *meris* meant only "share," not "district." But excavations in the Fayum of Egypt have shown that the colonists (many of whom came from Macedonia) used the word *meris* to talk about the political divisions in their district.

With respect to the political magistrates of the Roman colony of Philippi, Luke calls them *strategoi* (Greek word for the Latin *praetores*). While scholars used to insist that Luke used an incorrect term here (the correct Latin term would be *duoviri*), inscriptions found at Philippi indicate that *praetores* was indeed a popular designation for these magistrates.

Scholars have also suggested that Luke used the wrong term, *politarches*, to refer to the city officials at Thessalonica. But once again, a discovery of at least seventeen inscriptions at Salonika (modern Thessalonica) have demonstrated that this was indeed the correct term.

In fact, scholars today have to admit that Luke is entirely accurate in how he uses terminology for the political geography and officials of the ancient world. This may seem amazing, since some places changed terminology as the Roman government changed its administration of various cities and provinces. But to believers convinced of the infallibility of Scripture, this characteristic of Luke's writing is something to be expected.

One of the most important figures in Luke is Gallio, the Roman proconsul of Achaia before whom Paul stood on trial (Acts 18:12–16). This individual has become an anchor-point for Pauline chronology, since a stone fragment found at Delphi, fifty miles northwest of Corinth, contains an inscription from the emperor Claudius (dated somewhere between summer 51 to summer 52), which reads, in part: "[Concerning] the present stories and those quarrels of the citizens ... [a report has been made by Lucius] Junius Gallio, my friend and proconsul [for Achaea]." A Roman senator was proconsul generally for only a one-year term. In other words, most likely early in Gallio's term as proconsul, this confrontation took place (A.D. 51); Paul left Corinth to return to Jerusalem and Antioch in the spring of A.D. 52.

Paul's Third Missionary Journey

On Paul's third missionary journey, he spent most of his time in the city of Ephesus. He stayed there for three years—his longest stay anywhere. This city was fourth in population in the empire, behind Rome, Alexandria in Egypt, and Antioch of Syria. Certainly Paul must have felt that if he could make a significant impact on this city, he would make a significant impact on all of Asia Minor. Much excavation has been done in this area.

It is well known from history that Ephesus had one of the seven wonders of the ancient world, the temple to Artemis (see Acts 19:27, 35–36). In the mid- to late-nineteenth century, this temple was excavated. It was enormous, to say the least: The platform on which it stood was 239 feet wide, 418 feet long (more than 100 feet longer and wider than a modern football field). The temple itself was 180 feet wide and 377 feet long. It stood sixty feet high, with its roof supported by 117 columns, each of which was six feet in diameter. More than one-fourth of them had life-sized sculptured figures at their base.

Other excavations at Ephesus have uncovered small statuettes of Artemis, showing the multi-breasted goddess of Asia Minor. Also excavated, at the base on Mount Pion, is the amphitheater where Demetrius and his cohorts ended up after they managed to start the riot that was designed to protect their shrine industry. This massive outdoor structure, measuring 495 feet in diameter, seated up to 24,000 people. Anyone visiting the site today can imagine what the scene must have looked like during Paul's stay there.

A person sitting at the top of the theater could look down along the Arcadian Way, a thirty-six-foot-wide road that led to the harbor (now silted into dry land), with shops on both sides of it. Presumably from this harbor Paul set sail for Macedonia after the riot (Acts 20:1), stopping first at Troas (2 Cor. 2:12).

Paul's Arrest and Imprisonment

After Paul's third missionary journey he went to Jerusalem, delivering the collection he had been gathering from his Gentile churches for the poor among the saints in the holy city. As a political tactic to pacify the Judaizers, Paul agreed to undergo a Nazirite vow and to pay for the expenses of the purification rites of four others.

While Paul was going about his business, some Jews from Ephesus saw him and were convinced that he had allowed Trophimus, a Greek Christian from Ephesus, to go into one of the inner courts of the temple; they therefore started a riot (Acts 21:27–29). If true, this would have been a dangerous situation. At thirteen different spots around this inner court were signs that read: "Let no Gentile enter within the balustrade and enclosure surrounding the sanctuary. Whoever is caught will be personally responsible for his subsequent death." Archaeologists have found at least two of these notices.

When the riot started, soldiers quickly came to seize control. At the northwest corner of the temple complex stood the Antonia Fortress. Roman soldiers were garrisoned there, and the Roman governor was able to look over the entire temple complex and see any trouble spots immediately. After his arrest, Paul was imprisoned in this building.

What Luke records about the various people connected with Paul's imprisonment receives confirmation from historical sources. The high priest at the time, Ananias ben Nebedeus, was known to have a cruel streak (cf. Acts 23:2). Felix, a governor who had powerful connections in Rome, used extortion, cruelty, and oppression in Palestine, which may in part account for the rebellion of the Jews that led to the Jewish War. He was well informed about Christianity because his present wife was Drusilla, a Jewish woman (Acts 24:22–24).

One of the most realistic sections of the New Testament is the voyage and shipwreck of the apostle Paul as he was heading to Rome for his trial before Nero. The different winds and storms that Luke records still blow in the fall time in the Mediterranean Sea.

When Paul entered Rome, Nero had, it seems, just left the city because of the murder of his mother, most likely at the instigation of Nero himself. To escape the Roman populace's wrath at matricide, Nero disappeared for the next eighteen months. That may be why Paul's trial did not take place for at least two years after his arrival in Rome (cf. Acts 28:30–31).

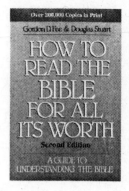
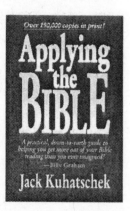

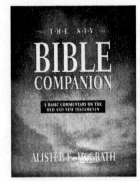

More books by John Sailhamer

The NIV Compact Series

This four-volume series sits handsomely on your desk or bookshelf, ready to answer your Bible study questions quickly and authoritatively. If you read the NIV Bible, then you need this series.

NIV Compact Concordance, by John R. Kohlenberger III and Edward W. Goodrick

    0-310-59480-4

NIV Compact Bible Commentary,
by John Sailhamer
    0-310-51460-6

NIV Compact Nave's Topical Bible,
by John R. Kohlenberger III
0-310-40210-7

NIV Compact Dictionary of the Bible,
by J. D. Douglas and Merrill C. Tenney
0-310-33180-3

The Pentateuch as Narrative
A Biblical-Theological Commentary

Understand the first five books of the Bible as their author originally intended. Dr. Sailhamer presents the Pentateuch as a coherent whole, revealing historical and literary themes that appear clearly only when it is read this way. A fresh look at the beginnings of the nation of Israel and the earliest foundations of the Christian faith.

Softcover: 0-310-57421-8

Available at your local Christian bookstore.

ZONDERVAN
.com

We want to hear from you. Please send your comments about this book to us in care of the address below. Thank you.

ZONDERVAN.com/
AUTHORTRACKER
follow your favorite authors